THE AMERICAS IN 1988

A Time for Choices

A Report of the
Inter-American Dialogue

Library of Congress Cataloging-in-Publication Data

Inter-American Dialogue (Organization)
The Americas in 1988.

1. Latin America—Economic conditions—1945—
2. Latin America—Economic policy. 3. Latin America—
Politics and government—1980–   . 4. Debts,
External—Latin America. 5. Latin America—Emigration
and immigration. 6. United States—Emigration and
immigration. 7. Drug traffic—Latin America. 8. Drug
traffic—United States. 9. Latin America—Armed
Forces—Political activity. I. Title.
HC125.I524   1988   330.98'038   88–17146
ISBN 0–8191–7083–6 (pbk. : alk. paper)
ISBN 0–8191–7082–8 (alk. paper)

Inter-American Dialogue

Since 1982, the Inter-American Dialogue has brought together concerned citizens from the United States, Canada, Latin America, and the Caribbean to review and make recommendations for action on hemispheric issues. At a time of deep strain in official U.S.-Latin American relations, the Dialogue plays two important roles: it offers a significant non-governmental channel of communication among leaders from throughout the Americas, and it provides sustained analysis and specific policy proposals to deal with key regional problems.

The chairmen of the Dialogue are Sol M. Linowitz, former U.S. Ambassador to the Organization of American States and co-negotiator of the Panama Canal Treaties, and Daniel Oduber, former president of Costa Rica. Other participants include two former Latin American presidents; more than a dozen former cabinet officers from the United States and Latin America; and business, labor, academic, media, military, and religious leaders. To assure frank discussion, all members participate as individuals, acting in their personal capacities. Persons currently exercising national government responsibility are not invited to join the Dialogue during their term in office.

Independent and non-partisan, the Inter-American Dialogue operates under the auspices of the Aspen Institute for Humanistic Studies, with financial support from foundations, international organizations, corporations, and individuals. The Dialogue has met in plenary session five times and has issued three previous reports—**The Americas at a Crossroads** (April 1983);

The Americas in 1984: A Year of Decisions (May 1984); and **Rebuilding Cooperation in the Americas** (April 1986). Copies of this year's report can be obtained by writing to:

> **The Inter-American Dialogue**
> **1333 New Hampshire Avenue, N.W.**
> **Suite 1070**
> **Washington, D.C. 20036**
>
> **Telephone: (202) 466-6410**

The Americas in 1988: A Time for Choices

A Report of the Inter-American Dialogue

May 1988
Aspen Institute for Humanistic Studies, Washington, D.C.

Executive Summary

Overview

● In recent months, debates on Central America have tended to fix blame more than to build peace. Now it is time to focus on how to help Central Americans build a better future. Specific measures must be taken to protect the national security of all Central American countries, promote national reconciliation and peaceful political competition, assist more than two million refugees, and reconstruct the region's shattered economies. (Chapter I)

● After six years, Latin America remains mired in debt, and there is still no consensus on how to restore economic growth in the region. Most creditor governments and institutions continue to support the Baker plan, while Latin American debtor nations increasingly see debt relief as the only way out of their economic bind. A majority of the Dialogue members favors debt relief—but some others consider it impractical and ultimately harmful to debtors and creditors alike, and would stick to the Baker approach. All of us, however, join in proposing a series of concrete actions to prevent Latin America from losing yet another decade of development. (Chapter II)

● Drug abuse—and associated crime and corruption—has reached staggering proportions in the Americas. Eradication, interdiction, and other supply-side policies have failed. Primary attention must now be given to curbing demand. The United States, particularly, should be spending more on education and rehabilitation. Producing countries should be encouraged to develop their own drug strategies, not pressured to impose U.S.-mandated solutions.   (Chapter III)

● Expanding populations, economic depression and political violence in Central America have vastly increased the flows of migrants within the Hemisphere. These flows have, in turn, produced heightened opposition to immigration in the United States and other countries. Migrants and refugees deserve better treatment throughout the Americas. The 1986 U.S. immigration law needs to be improved, particularly so that larger numbers of undocumented aliens would become eligible for legal residence. The United States should also consider special migration arrangements with Mexico, recognizing the strong economic interdependence of the two countries. (Chapter IV)

● Latin America's new democracies are menaced by an old enemy: the danger of military intervention in politics. Unless new patterns of civil-military relations can be firmly established, a new round of military coups may occur in the 1990s. Concrete measures must be taken to strengthen civilian control, inculcate new political attitudes in the region's armed forces, and help assure that foreign military training programs strengthen, not weaken, democracy. (Chapter V)

Chapter I: Central America: A Vision of Peace

Peace is not yet at hand in Central America, but the August 1987 Accord among the five Central American presidents has produced more progress toward peace in the past several months than was achieved during the previous seven years.

The Accord provides a framework and process to end the region's conflicts based on three principles: non-aggression among governments of Central America, a withdrawal of external support for insurgencies, and respect for political freedoms under each country's constitution. This framework can lead to peace.

In recent months, debates on Central America have done more to fix blame than to build peace. It is now time to focus on what kind of future Central Americans want, and what others in the Hemisphere can do to help.

Four intertwined problems need to be confronted:

● All the countries of the region must be assured that their national security will be protected. The countries of Central America should prohibit foreign military bases on their territory, limit sharply the number of foreign military advisers, and curtail arms acquisitions. The United States should negotiate directly with the Soviet Union and Nicaragua to reduce Soviet military presence and bar advanced weapons systems from the region. The Guatemala Accord's ban on support for insurgent forces must be enforced. The United States must confine further aid to the Contras to genuinely humanitarian assistance for the purpose of reintegrating them into normal life. Nicaragua must cease all military and paramilitary support for insurgent movements elsewhere.

Governments and insurgent movements in Central America should strive to convert their military strife into peaceful political competition. Nicaragua, El Salvador, and Guatemala must convince guerrilla forces in their countries that laying down their arms will open the way for full participation in national affairs. These governments have to allow their opponents to organize openly and compete freely in elections at all levels. Persistent international support for freedom of expression and association can help to expand political space. Concerted, symmetric, and reciprocal pressures are more likely than armed attack or mere exhortation to pave the way toward national reconciliation, pluralist politics, and democracy.

● Throughout Central America, adequate steps must be taken to assist refugees to reintegrate into their societies or to relocate permanently. Central American refugees should be granted safe haven in the countries where they now reside, and provided with emergency assistance for food, medical care, education, housing, and legal services. A special problem requiring sensitive treatment is the fate of the Nicaraguan Contras. As negotiations proceed to end the civil war, Nicaragua must be prepared to provide security guarantees and economic assistance to facilitate the return of all Contras willing to lay down their arms. Those who are ready to disarm but are not prepared to return to Nicaragua immediately should be helped to remain in Central America. The United States should offer to resettle Contra leaders and their families who are unwilling to return to Nicaragua.

● The economies of Central America must be rebuilt, expanded, and made more equitable. Beyond emergency relief, the international community should provide generous assistance to help rebuild infrastructure, expand the region's productive base, and improve social services. Industrial country creditors should offer improved access to their markets for Central America's exports and provide compensatory financing to the region when its export prices drop. Interest payments on Central America's official bilateral debt should be used to establish a special fund for regional reconstruction.

Chapter II: The Debt Trap: Still No Escape

Latin America has now been mired in debt and depression for six years. Yet there is still no firm consensus on how to resolve Latin America's debt problems and revive its damaged economies.

Most creditor governments and institutions continue to support the plan put forth by U.S. Treasury Secretary James Baker in 1985. Latin American governments, by and large, however, have lost confidence in the Baker plan— which has not produced the resources or results it promised. They are increasingly calling for debt relief to reduce the region's massive capital outflows.

A substantial majority— but not all— of the members of the Dialogue are ready to endorse debt relief for Latin American countries. Indeed, many Dialogue participants are persuaded that significant debt relief is virtually inevitable in light of recent economic and political developments.

● The region's overall debt has grown from $330 billion when the crisis began in 1982 to some $420 billion today. Despite a steep drop in interest rates since 1982, the all-important ratio of debt payments to export earnings has scarcely improved. Only a very few countries have made strides toward recovery, while most remain in deep economic slumps, with debt obligations draining away resources needed for investment.

• In many countries, the political forces calling for suspension of debt payments are gaining ground, while more moderate and pragmatic leaders are on the defensive. In November 1987, eight key Latin American presidents meeting in Mexico stressed that economic failure was imperilling progress toward democracy, and urged that debt service be reduced to each country's ability to pay.

• Finally, the international community is not providing the capital essential for recovery. Private banks have reduced, not expanded, their commitments to Latin America. Resource flows from international financial institutions have levelled off. Moreover, sluggish world growth and increasing protectionism hamper Latin America's efforts to expand trade.

We all recognize the serious obstacles to debt relief: the heavy costs it would impose on commercial banks; the possible disincentives for sound debtor country policies; Latin America's potential loss of private financing over the longer term; and, most importantly, the lack of political support in the industrialized countries for making the necessary resources available. Most of us, however, think that these obstacles can be overcome, and that the central question is not whether debt relief is justified or necessary, but how to bring it about in the most constructive and orderly way.

Some Dialogue members, however, see debt relief as impractical and ultimately harmful to the interests of debtors and creditors alike. They recognize the weaknesses and poor performance of the Baker plan—but believe it can be sufficiently fortified to achieve its objectives of policy reform, increased capital flows, and, ultimately, satisfactory growth in Latin America.

Despite these differences, all Dialogue members agree on these fundamental points:

• Concerted action is urgently needed to restore economic expansion of at least five percent a year to Latin America—to avoid political disaffection and renew public confidence in democratic governments.

● Every country of Latin America must adopt sound economic policies as part of a development program agreed upon with its creditors.

● International financial institutions and official export credit agencies must significantly step up their lending to Latin America.

● Commercial banks and official creditors should grant explicit debt relief to Latin America's weakest performing economies, most of which cannot pay their current obligations.

● For those countries not granted debt relief, commercial banks should be called on to provide substantially more capital— and to do so expeditiously.

● Creditors and debtors should jointly establish specific targets for each country's external financing needs. Countries that adhere to economic reform programs but still face persistent shortfalls in new financing should be allowed to defer interest payments to make up the differences.

● If these measures do not provide enough financing to revive Latin America's economies, concessional debt relief may well be necessary for a growing number of countries.

If Latin America does not escape from the debt trap soon, the region's governments may increasingly turn away from cooperative approaches toward unilateral action to deal with their economic problems. This would carry a high price for both creditors and debtors. Latin America's development would be set back, not advanced, and the region might face another lost decade.

Chapter III: Drugs: A Shared Tragedy
The gap between drug abuse in the Hemisphere and government responses grows ever wider. The U.S. Administration has declared a war on drugs, and between 1982 and 1987, Washington's spending for drug law enforcement tripled, to nearly $3 billion. Arrests and seizures are both up, and marijuana eradication in the United States jumped

ten-fold from 1984 to 1986. Moreover, the Anti-Drug Abuse Act of 1986 now authorizes a variety of pressures on Latin American drug producing countries.

Abroad, in 1986, helicopter-borne U.S. military and law enforcement personnel raided cocaine laboratories in Bolivia. Due in part to U.S. pressure, more than half of the Mexican Attorney General's 1987 budget was spent on drug crop eradication, and in 1986, Colombia increased its marijuana eradication efforts by 50 percent.

The results? Illegal narcotics are more plentiful in the United States than ever, with cocaine prices today at one-third of 1984 levels. Among high school seniors, the incidence of cocaine smoking shot up from 2.5 percent to 6 percent. In all, narcotics sales in the United States total an estimated $100 billion annually—more than twice what was spent on oil. And marijuana is now the second largest U.S. cash crop. At the same time, drug abuse has been rising rapidly throughout much of Latin America and the Caribbean—compounding, as it does in the United States, other social ills: poverty, crime, poor schools, and erosion of authority.

The world supply of coca leaf is estimated to have doubled in the last four years. More and more Latin American countries are becoming part of the narcotics network. Coca cultivation, for example, once limited to Peru and Bolivia, has now spread to half a dozen other countries. Nearly 15 countries are involved in the production, processing and distribution of cocaine. And as drug trafficking has spread, so has the crime and corruption associated with it. The institutions of representative government—judicial systems, police and military forces, and local and national bureaucracies—are under siege in many countries.

Supply-side policies, like eradication and interdiction, have failed to stem the drug menace. Primary attention must now shift to curbing demand. The United States must take the lead by funding prevention, education, and rehabilitation programs more generously, and sponsoring more research to make those programs work better. Financing for such efforts has hardly increased since 1981. It may also be useful to consider approaches that distinguish among different drugs, and differentiate between the damage caused by drug abuse and the harm produced by their illegality. It is premature to contemplate legalizing any dangerous drug, but it might be sensible to examine carefully the likely consequences, positive and negative, of selective legislation.

The United States should stop trying to force eradication programs on Latin American governments, and stop threatening sanctions for inadequate cooperation. This policy has antagonized other countries and may risk discrediting U.S. anti-drug efforts generally. Instead, Washington should help producing countries develop their own drug strategies that represent national choices, not concessions to foreign pressure.

The drug problem will not be solved quickly or easily. No nation, by itself, can find a solution, and all nations must avoid inflated rhetoric and finger pointing. Narcotics are not alone on the hemispheric agenda. Friction over narcotics should not be allowed to hamper cooperation on other critical problems.

Chapter IV: Migration: Problem or Solution?

Expanding populations, economic depression, and Central American strife have vastly increased international migration within the Hemisphere. Opposition to the resulting flows, in turn, has heightened in the United States and other countries.

Most migration to the Americas is propelled by economic considerations— by the promise of better jobs and higher wages. By far the largest flow is from Mexico to the United States. In recent years, political violence and repression have combined with economic distress to produce new migration streams. More than two million Central Americans have been displaced from their homes; more than half of them have fled to other countries. Government oppression and desperate poverty have also created massive migration from Haiti.

The Hemisphere's piecemeal response to the problems of both labor migrants and refugees has been inadequate. Migration policy measures should be set cooperatively, not simply determined unilaterally by recipient countries. The United States, for example, should begin to review the issues posed by its new immigration law with countries of origin who fear that it may threaten their economic and political stability. But sending countries must also consider changing domestic economic and political policies that produce large numbers of migrants.

The U.S. immigration law needs improvement. Undocumented aliens who may be eligible for amnesty under the law should be given more time to apply, and the amnesty program should be broadened to allow others to qualify. Washington should also open legal avenues for mutually beneficial economic migration. The United States should explore special immigration arrangements with Mexico because of the great economic interdependence of the two societies.

Mexico and the United States together should ease their restrictions on Central American migrants by expanding eligibility for political asylum, suspending routine deportations, and permitting the permanent resettlement of Central Americans who have lived in their territories for three years or more. The countries of the region, meanwhile, should also allow for the resettlement of refugees who cannot or will not return to their native lands.

Ultimately, every nation of the Hemisphere must decide for itself what it means for an individual or family to "belong" to its society, and how to deal with the situation of people who are physically present but barred from full social and political participation. Each country must balance its interest in discouraging unwanted migration with the need to integrate newcomers. For the Americas as a whole, migration can be managed effectively only if nations and governments face up to the fact that large-scale flows of people will mark hemispheric life for decades to come. With cooperative and jointly formulated policies that address the needs of sending and receiving societies and of the migrants themselves, migration can enrich every nation of the Hemisphere— and bind us all closer together.

Chapter V: Preserving Democracy:
The Military Challenge

Latin America's regionwide turn toward democracy has gained important ground in the 1980s, but it remains menaced by an old enemy: military intervention in politics. The 1988 crisis in Panama illustrates that threat in a very special form, but the problem is widespread. Unless new patterns of civil-military relations can be established, a new round of military coups may well plague Latin America in the 1990s.

The three main sources of civil-military tensions are: government efforts to curb the military's authority and privileges; civilian attempts to prosecute military officers for human rights violations; and disagreements over how to respond to guerilla insurgencies.

So far, such tensions have not produced any outright military coups. These have been forestalled by military awareness of the damage done to the armed forces during previous periods of rule, by public opposition to a return to military rule, and by international support for democratic governments. But this respite may not last. Latin America's prolonged economic crisis is weakening the authority of civilian leaders and could lead to calls for the military to take power once again. Anti-democratic attitudes remain strong in some sectors, and these are fed by continued civilian deference to military demands for autonomy and privilege. If concerted efforts are not made throughout Latin America to restructure civilian-military relations, democracy in the region could falter.

Above all else, reducing the risk of military intervention requires that civilian governments be strengthened. The current imbalances between weak political institutions and strong military establishments must be overcome. Civilian leaders must gain clear authority to make foreign and defense policy, establish military budgets and force levels, and set the rules that govern the armed forces and their relations with the rest of society.

Democratic governments must also develop strategies for changing the attitudes of military officers about their proper political role and for integrating the armed forces within democratic regimes. An effort must be undertaken to change military thinking about internal security and subversion. The military cannot consider itself the ultimate guardian of national values, or insist that national security embraces all aspects of policy. Military education must be reformed to strengthen civilian control of politics.

Important changes in civilian attitudes are needed as well to diminish prospects of military intervention in government. Civilian politicians have to resist the temptation to seek the military's help in resolving political conflicts or in gaining national power.

A first critical step toward improving civil-military relations is to establish a continuing dialogue among civilian and military leaders. Public and private forums should be organized to encourage such dialogue on the full range of outstanding issues.

All the Hemisphere's democratic governments should consistently express their support for constitutional democracy: diplomatically, politically, and economically. Greater efforts should be made to reinforce the message that constitutional democracy is vital for hemispheric security. External military assistance or training should be provided only to countries where these will not weaken democratic politics, but rather help defend them from attack. U.S. programs have trained over 100,000 Latin American soldiers since 1950, but they have often failed to ingrain desirable norms about democracy and civilian supremacy. Canada and the Scandinavian countries may provide more relevant role models for Latin American militaries and should be encouraged to expand their training programs in the region. External military training programs should not be reserved for military officers alone; they should also include Latin American civilians involved in defense and military policy.

# Preface

1988 is a year of fateful anticipation throughout the Americas, North and South.

A new administration will take over early next year in Washington. Presidential elections are also due soon in four of Latin America's largest nations—Brazil, Mexico, Argentina, and Venezuela—and in a number of others as well. These changes in national leadership will inevitably transform the Hemisphere's political map.

Not only are leaders changing, but the agenda of inter-American relations is also in flux. The major problems of the 1980s are still with us, but their nature is shifting, and new issues are emerging.

- The strategy for coping with Latin America's massive debt has prevented financial chaos, but the inadequacies of that strategy have become painfully clear. It has not restored sustained growth in Latin America, and many doubt that it ever will.

- Throughout the 1980s, out attention was fixed on the civil wars in Central America. These have not yet been settled, but now there is hope that political reconciliation and economic reconstruction may soon become the main challenges in that troubled region.

- The key issue in the early 1980s for South America was how to replace authoritarian military regimes with constitutional democracies. That goal has been accomplished in all but two countries. Now fragile civilian regimes must be strengthened to assure their survival.

- In recent years, inter-American institutions have atrophied badly, yet Latin American countries have been cooperating among themselves far more than previously. These collective efforts could provide the basis for renewed inter-American cooperation—or they could produce heightened confrontation between Latin America and the United States.

This fourth report of the Inter-American Dialogue focuses on the Hemisphere's mounting frustrations and the dangers they pose to U.S.-Latin American relations. The prolonged economic crisis of the 1980s has exacted a particularly high price. The region has lost a full decade of growth while the demands of an expanding population have multiplied. Central America's wars have ground on: killing, maiming, and displacing thousands of people and destroying much of that region's productive capacity. The drug curse, infecting both North and South America, has grown to dimensions no one imagined ten years ago. Migration flows, long viewed as a positive feature of the Americas, have become so large that exclusionist sentiments have been aroused in many places.

Economic difficulties, military forces outside of civilian control, drugs, and guerrilla insurgencies are making it difficult for new democratic governments to establish their credibility and retain popular backing. In many countries, moderate and pragmatic leaders are losing support to those advocating more extremist policies. What is at stake is much more than confidence in specific leaders; it is the legitimacy of democratic rule itself.

One basic proposition clearly emerges from our analysis: unilateral approaches, whether undertaken by the United States or by any of the nations of Latin America, are the wrong way to deal with hemispheric problems. Such approaches are mostly ineffective in addressing the problems and are usually damaging to inter-American relations generally.

The 1988 crisis in Panama is a dramatic illustration. Unilateral U.S. economic sanctions and other pressures

xx

against Panama have hindered efforts by Latin American and European leaders to promote a negotiated end to Panama's crisis and mobilized widespread Latin American resentment to U.S. policy.

These past years have shown what cooperation among the countries of the Hemisphere can accomplish. The outstanding example is the Central American peace process launched by President Oscar Arias Sánchez of Costa Rica—and then joined by the region's other four presidents. The progress they have made, in turn, would not have been possible without the ground-breaking work of the four Contadora nations and the support group of four South American democracies.

Our report also underscores the futility of seeking "quick fixes" for major hemispheric problems. Whether the issue is curbing the drug trade, coping with large-scale movements of people, fostering reconciliation in fractured societies, or rebuilding damaged economies—the essential ingredients are time, patience and persistence. There will always be political demands for quick solutions, but sound approaches take time to work.

Since 1982, the Inter-American Dialogue has sought to improve the quality of attention given to inter-American problems and to promote cooperative solutions to shared problems. Our members come from many different countries and bring many diverse professional and political perspectives, but we all share a deep concern for hemispheric relations. We are committed to exploring our differences frankly, searching hard for areas of agreement, and offering constructive recommendations.

This report is a group effort. Not every signer agrees fully with every statement in the report, but all affirm that the document reflects the consensus of the Dialogue's participants. Except as noted by individual statements appended to the text, each of us subscribes to the report's overall content and tone, and supports its principal recommendations.

The signers of the report take sole responsibility for it. The report does not necessarily represent the views of the foundations, international institutions, individuals, or corporations that have supported the Dialogue; the various organizations with which the signers are affiliated; or the Aspen Institute for Humanistic Studies, under whose auspices the Dialogue operates.

The Inter-American Dialogue draws on the help of many people and institutions. We owe particular gratitude to Peter D. Bell and Rodrigo Botero, the Dialogue's co-vice chairmen, and to the other members of the Executive Committee. We also express our great appreciation to the Dialogue's staff: Abraham F. Lowenthal of the University of Southern California, executive director; Peter Hakim, full time staff director in Washington; Yasmin Santiago, executive assistant; and Geoffrey Pyatt and Louellen Stedman, associates.

We are grateful as well to Edmar Bacha, J. Samuel Fitch, Victor C. Johnson, Doris Meissner, Gabriel Murillo, Luis Pásara, Gregory F. Treverton, and Viron P. Vaky for their major contributions to the Dialogue's work during the past year; to the many other persons who prepared background papers and memoranda and contributed advice; to Jill Schuker and John Trattner for their help on communications; to Zaida Knight for translation services; Alan Tonelson for editorial assistance; and Marge Fitzgerald, Karen Pokraka and Virginia Schofield for administrative assistance.

We thank the Secretary General of the Organization of American States, João Clemente Baena Soares, for generously hosting the reception following our plenary meeting and for sharing his ideas with us; the many ambassadors and government officials who contributed their thoughts; and staff members of the World Bank, the Inter-American Development Bank, the Economic Commission on Latin America and the Caribbean, and the Organization of American States who provided advice.

We express our special gratitude to the Aspen Institute for its strong support and many important contributions to the Dialogue's work. We are indebted as well to the Carnegie Endowment for International Peace, the Peruvian Center of International Studies, the Institute of the Americas, the Helen Kellogg Institute at the University of Notre Dame, and the Corporation for Latin American Economic Research (CIEPLAN) for their sustained cooperation in our work.

We very much appreciate the major financial support the Dialogue has received from the Ford, William and Flora Hewlett, John D. and Catherine MacArthur, and Rockefeller Foundations and the Carnegie Corporation of New York. We are also grateful for contributions by the International Development Research Centre, the World Bank, the William Farley Foundation, IBM-Americas/Far East Corporation, the Marine Midland Bank, the ARCA Foundation, and several individual donors.

The Dialogue began in 1982 with the encouragement and active leadership of Galo Plaza, the former president of Ecuador and Secretary General of the Organization of American States, who served as co-chairman until his death early in 1987. Galo Plaza had many unforgettable qualities: intelligence and grace; deep concern for people of all types and classes; and the gift of leadership that is captured in the Spanish phrase "don de mando." But no quality of Galo Plaza's was more remarkable than his abiding and unswerving commitment to cooperation in the Americas. He helped shape the Dialogue and our continuing work together honors his memory.

Sol M. Linowitz
Daniel Oduber
Co-Chairmen
April 28, 1988

Dialogue Co-chairman Daniel Oduber

Dialogue Co-chairman Sol M. Linowitz

Chapter I

Central America: A Vision of Peace

After years of bitter fighting, Central America today has a hazy vision of peace.

For more than a decade, Central America has been wracked by armed struggles in El Salvador, Guatemala, and Nicaragua. These conflicts have involved all the countries of the region and several outside the isthmus. Central America's profound economic, social and political problems—the root causes of civil strife—have become all the more difficult.

Yet there is now hope in Central America that the region's agony can be ended. Violence, poverty, and repression still prevail, but for the first time in years there is the prospect of a better future. This promise can only be realized, however, if the many participants in Central America's turmoil persevere, despite risks and disappointments, in quest of peace.

A Tragic Decade

Central America's fighting has taken a terrible toll. Guatemala's fierce bloodletting during the 1960s, 1970s and early 1980s took many tens of thousands of lives and left that nation in trauma. Some 50,000 persons have died in Nicaragua's strife since 1978, the equivalent of nearly five million deaths in a country the size of the United States. There have been even more casualties in El Salvador, where shifting military tactics by both the guerrillas and the Army have become ever more destructive. At least 3,000 persons were killed or wounded in the Salvadoran war just during the past year.

Altogether, Central America's struggles have killed nearly 200,000 people during the last 15 years, and have injured scores of thousands of others. More than two million Central Americans have been displaced from their homes; almost half of these have fled their own countries for refuge elsewhere in the region or beyond. A generation of Central America's youth has grown up accepting pervasive violence as a cruel fact of life.

Central America's economies have been badly hurt. War has destroyed much of the physical infrastructure of El Salvador and Nicaragua. Property losses alone have been estimated at several billion dollars. The region has diverted increasingly scarce resources to preparing for war, making war, and repairing the damage it causes. Nicaragua spends over half of its national budget on defense, thus fueling unmanageable inflationary pressures. El Salvador's army has swelled from 10,000 men in 1980 to some 54,000 today. The military hardware coming into Central America is every year more destructive and costly. Even in Honduras and Costa Rica, which have been spared open conflict, the region's militarization has heightened economic and political stress.

Falling commodity prices have sharply reduced Central America's export earnings, but the region's wars have blocked economic diversification. The once-promising trend toward regional integration, slowed for economic reasons in the 1970s, has been reversed by war in the 1980s. Foreign investment in Central America has dried up, local investment has dwindled, tourism has stopped (except in Costa Rica), and capital flight has soared. Per capita production and income have plummeted during the 1980s, in some countries to levels of the 1960s. Throughout the region, poverty and deprivation are more widespread than they were a decade ago. Increased external aid—mainly from the United States to El Salvador, Honduras, Guatemala, and Costa Rica and from the socialist bloc and Western Europe to Nicaragua—has only managed to slow the region's decline.

Beyond the casualties, the destruction of property, and the economic deterioration, Central America has suffered during the 1980s in a less tangible but most painful way: the social and political cohesion of these small countries (again, but for Costa Rica) has been undermined.

Struggles for power and influence have escalated into questions of life and death. Distrust and hostility have badly divided families, groups, and organizations. Few persons or institutions, with the important exception of the Catholic Church, still command widespread respect.

Vision of Peace

Central America remains a region at war. Since August 1987, however, many Central Americans have begun to glimpse the image of peace. They capture this vision in a single word— *Esquipulas*— the name of the small town in Guatemala where the region's five presidents first convened in May 1986 to revive the stalled Central American peace process.

When all five presidents reconvened in Guatemala in August 1987 to discuss the peace plan offered by Costa Rican President Oscar Arias Sánchez, what happened was dramatic. Despite mistrust and antagonism among the presidents, the five persisted in their discussions until together they had drafted and signed the "Procedure for the Establishment of a Firm and Lasting Peace in Central America." This soon became known as the Guatemala Accord, or more commonly in Latin America, Esquipulas II.

Among its provisions, the Guatemala Accord established joint commitments among the Central American governments to seek cease-fires in the region's armed conflicts; to promote democracy by lifting states of emergency, allowing media freedom, and re-establishing constitutional guarantees; and to foster national reconciliation by providing amnesties and initiating dialogues with opposition movements. The presidents promised not to allow their countries' territories to be used by insurgent groups battling other governments. They requested countries outside the region to stop aiding insurrectionist movements. Looking toward the future, they pledged to facilitate the repatriation or resettlement of refugees and displaced persons; to seek jointly international support for Central America's reconstruction and development; and to negotiate with each other on arms reduction and other military issues. To resolve outstanding security questions, the presidents agreed to work within the Contadora framework established by Mexico, Colombia, Venezuela, and Panama, which have been promoting a negotiated solution in Central America since 1983.

The Accord also called for the establishment of National Reconciliation Commissions in each country to mediate civil strife and verify compliance with negotiated commitments. It mandated the creation of an International Commission on Verification and Follow-Up to encourage and evaluate adherence to the Accord. The Commission was composed of representatives of the Secretaries General of the United Nations and the Organization of American States, together with the Foreign Ministers of all five Central American countries and of eight other Latin American nations: the original Contadora four plus the "Support Group" of Argentina, Brazil, Peru and Uruguay. The Accord included other procedures and deadlines to promote implementation of its provisions.

Throughout Central America and beyond the region, the Guatemala Accord was greeted as a major breakthrough. Few had expected the five presidents to agree on specific aims, commitments, and timetables for a peace settlement. That they did so sparked hope that political opening and reconciliation might still be possible.

The Guatemala Accord did not end the deep hostility within and among the Central American nations, however, nor did it stop the armed struggles. On the contrary, fighting intensified in Nicaragua, El Salvador and Guatemala as the contending armies vied for immediate advantage. It became clear that the five presidents had little more than diplomatic and political means to compel each other to pursue the announced goals.

Yet the Guatemala Accord produced some remarkable changes. For the first time since the region's conflicts broke out, Nicaraguans and Salvadorans, both from governments and from insurgent oppositions, began seriously to contemplate the prospect of peace. As the deadlines for implementation and evaluation approached, the five presidents engaged in an unprecedented set of negotiations—formal and informal, international and domestic.

In the wake of the Guatemala Accord, every Central American government and the various insurgent movements took important steps toward peace:

- In El Salvador, a political amnesty freed several hundred alleged guerrillas and supporters of the insurgency, and nearly 4,500 refugees returned to their homes from neighboring Honduras. The government and the insurgents resumed their long-suspended talks. The two most prominent exiled opposition leaders visited the country to assess the climate for open political activity, and peaceful demonstrations and other opposition activities intensified.

- In Guatemala, government officials met for the first time in 27 years with representatives of the country's insurgent movements. Soon thereafter, a small delegation of political exiles visited Guatemala City to test the possibilities for expressing political dissent.

- In Honduras, where there is no significant armed insurgency and the country's politics are relatively open, the government declared much of the Guatemala Accord non-applicable. But Honduras did name a National Reconciliation Commission (which initiated a dialogue with opposition parties and other groups) and cooperated with international efforts to repatriate Salvadoran and Nicaraguan refugees. Although Honduras has not yet complied with the Accord's prohibition on the use of its territory by insurgent forces, President José Azcona promised to dismantle the remaining Contra camps in Honduras when a cease-fire is achieved in Nicaragua.

- Even Costa Rica, the most democratic and peaceful nation in the region, established a National Reconciliation Commission, which soon became a kind of national ombudsman and champion of human rights. Costa Rica also informed leaders of Nicaragua's armed resistance (the Contras) that they could no longer reside in Costa Rica if they continued to command a cross-border insurgency.

- Nicaragua, the country most distant from any regional consensus when the Central American peace process began, took a number of steps to implement the Guatemala Accord. It was the first nation to establish a National Reconciliation Commission; the Sandinistas appointed their most prominent Nicaraguan critic, Miguel Cardinal Obando y Bravo, the Archbishop of Managua, to head the Commission. Nicaragua freed nearly 1,000 prisoners; allowed the reopening of <u>La Prensa</u>, the country's major independent newspaper, and of Radio Católica; permitted several exiled priests to return; and resumed dialogues with dissident Indian groups. In early December 1987, the Nicaraguan government initiated indirect cease-fire negotiations with the Contras, reversing its long-standing refusal to negotiate at all with the U.S.-supported counter-revolutionary movement.

In mid-January 1988, when the five presidents reconvened in Costa Rica to review compliance with the Guatemala Accord, Nicaragua announced that it was lifting its state of emergency and restoring constitutional guarantees, and that it was willing to negotiate a cease-fire directly with the Contras. Nicaragua also promised to release all political prisoners once a cease-fire was achieved, or else to allow the prisoners to leave immediately for safe haven in any country outside Central America.

Direct negotiations with the contras soon began, first outside Nicaragua and then, in March 1988, at Sapoá, on Nicaraguan soil. On March 24, 1988, Sandinista and Contra leaders reached agreement on a 60-day truce, during which they would negotiate a permanent cease-fire, to "be carried out jointly with the other commitments contemplated in the Esquipulas II agreement." The Sandinista government, for its part, gave new assurances of political openings and promised a gradual amnesty for political prisoners, even for former members of Somoza's National Guard. The rebels, meanwhile, agreed to concentrate in designated cease-fire zones, where they are permitted to receive only humanitarian aid, channelled through neutral organizations.

All the steps taken toward peace and political opening in Central America have been limited and reversible. Indeed, some setbacks have occurred. Although the negotiations between Nicaragua's government and the Contras have progressed, attempts to undercut the talks have been made by partisans on both sides, and the dialogue between the Sandinistas and the internal opposition has made little headway. The negotiations between the governments of El Salvador and Guatemala and the insurgents in those countries have not been productive, as mediators and reconciliation commissions have been denounced and extreme positions advanced as ultimatums. The fighting in El Salvador persists; the levels of armaments and casualties have actually mounted during the past year; and the country has become even more polarized. Political violence has also increased in Guatemala and Honduras. The plight of refugees throughout the region has gone mostly unattended. Violations of human rights are still common in every country but Costa Rica, and little is being done to punish those who are responsible; amnesty programs have been used in Guatemala and El Salvador to spare death-squad killers from prosecution. It is by no means clear that all external military and paramilitary aid for insurgent and irregular forces has ceased.

Peace is not yet at hand in Central America, but the Guatemala Accord, for all its limitations, has produced more perceptible progress toward peace in Central America in a few months than had been achieved during the preceding seven years. Although definitive results have not yet been registered, a path has been opened. The Accord provides a framework and a process, built on three key principles: mutual acceptance and non-aggression among the existing governments of Central America, an end to external support for insurgencies, and respect for political freedoms under each country's constitution. This process is bound to encounter obstacles, and to advance at best by fits and starts, but we believe it can succeed.

Building on Esquipulas

In the months since the Guatemala Accord, attention in Washington and elsewhere in the Hemisphere has concentrated on the immediate accomplishments and frustrations of Central America's peace process. The prime focus has been shifting constantly from one short-run issue to another: the nature of the Reconciliation Commissions, the extent of media freedoms, the scope of cease-fire negotiations, and the question of aid to the Contras. We believe it is vital now, however, to look beyond these debates, which have tended more to fix blame than to build peace. It is time to focus on how to attain the kind of future Central Americans want, and what others in the Hemisphere can do to help.

For Central America to achieve and sustain peace, four intertwined problems need to be confronted:

- All the countries of Central America and the other countries of the Hemisphere must be assured that their national security and territorial integrity will not be threatened. Only if every nation of the Americas is protected from aggression, direct or indirect, can all nations be secure.

- The governments and the insurgent movements of Central America must try to convert their military strife into peaceful political competition. Only when all major social groups can safely contend for national power will the cycle of regional violence be broken.

- Throughout Central America, adequate steps must be taken to assist refugees to reintegrate into their societies or else to relocate permanently. The social and political fabric of Central America cannot be repaired while so many of the region's people remain displaced from their homes and normal sources of livelihood.

- The economies of Central America must be revived, expanded and made more equitable. Until this root cause of Central America's violence is addressed, there can be no lasting regional peace.

Each of these four challenges is daunting, for they amount to reversing the legacy of many years. All of them must be achieved to produce sustainable peace in Central America. There is no necessary sequence for achieving these goals; they should be vigorously addressed in tandem. Progress on any one dimension should not be held hostage to the others.

Constructing a Secure Peace

Central America's security depends ultimately on fashioning internal arrangements that allow all groups throughout the isthmus to participate fully in political life, thus gaining a stake in building civic peace. That is why Esquipulas focuses on national reconciliation and political opening, to establish the basis for lasting peace.

The most direct and immediate challenge to hemispheric security, however, arises from the tension between Nicaragua's Sandinista government and the other nations of the Americas—especially Nicaragua's neighbors in Central America and, farther away, the government of the United States. Nicaragua under the Sandinistas has disturbed the region's stability by its ideological commitment to revolution; its assistance to insurgent movements in other nations; and its military and political ties to the Soviet Union and Cuba.

Since 1981, the United States has prompted and supported the Contra war against Nicaragua, and several Central American nations have cooperated with the anti-Sandinista campaign. With massive help from the Soviet Union and Cuba, Nicaragua has substantially bolstered its armed strength. Nicaragua's military prowess has seemed menacing to neighboring countries, and they, in turn, have shored up their own armies. The resulting arms race has further heightened Central America's tensions. Insecurity has been exacerbated, moreover, by the escalating involvement in the region of both the United States and the Soviet Union.

Ending the tension between Nicaragua and its neighbors requires either that the Sandinista government be removed from power or that the security of all governments in the region be guaranteed.

Those who have favored ousting the Sandinista regime by force have promoted the Contra war for almost seven years. The war has killed many thousands of Nicaraguans and shattered the country's economy. Yet the Sandinistas remain in power, and are unlikely to lose their grip. The Sandinistas will not likely be dislodged by force, short of direct military intervention by the United States. There is very little support, within the United States or elsewhere in the Americas, for such an intervention, which would damage inter-American relations for years to come.

The Inter-American Dialogue has consistently opposed a military approach to what we see as a primarily political problem. We have emphasized the high cost of violating international law and regional norms. As we predicted in earlier reports, the Contra war has not led the Sandinistas to limit their arms build-up or loosen their ties with the Soviet Union and Cuba; in fact, the opposite has occurred.

It is high time to adopt the approach of Esquipulas, the search for a negotiated settlement in Central America. We believe that Nicaragua and its neighbors can co-exist in peace, despite their differences.

Nicaragua's main threat to hemispheric security arises from its connections to Soviet and Cuban military power, and from the potential that Cuba or the Soviet Union might try to use Nicaragua as a base for projecting hostile designs. What is most needed to protect security, therefore, is to reduce the Soviet and Cuban presence by using two mutually reinforcing approaches:

First, we urge the countries of Central America, as called for in the Guatemala Accord, to resume negotiations on security, arms limits, and verification within the framework of the Contadora draft treaty of June 1986. Nicaragua and its neighbors should agree to prohibit foreign military bases on their territories, limit sharply the number of foreign military advisors, and curtail arms acquisitions.

Second, the United States should negotiate directly with the Soviet Union and Nicaragua to protect its legitimate security interests. The United States should press for an immediate reduction in the Soviet military presence in Nicaragua, and should make clear that it would regard any increase in Soviet military aid as an unacceptable provocation, with consequences for other aspects of the bilateral relationship. The United States should continue to explore with the Soviet Union concrete ways to reduce superpower competition in Nicaragua and other Third World regions.

The United States should negotiate directly with Nicaragua to assure that advanced weapons systems that would destabilize the regional military balance will not be introduced. The United States should offer to reduce U.S. maneuvers and other manifestations of the U.S. military presence in Central America as the Soviet and Cuban presence is diminished. The United States should also make clear to Cuba that the prospects for regional peace depend on Cuba ending all support for insurgent movements, whether channeled through Nicaragua or otherwise.

A different security challenge is posed by Nicaragua's support for insurgent movements elsewhere in the region. Here the remedy is clear; the Guatemala Accord's ban on support for irregular or insurrectionary forces must be enforced. It is crucial that the United States confine its further aid to the Contras to genuinely humanitarian assistance for the purpose of reintegrating them into Nicaragua's normal life, as is contemplated in the Guatemala Accord and the Sapoá agreement. Nicaragua, too, must cease all military and paramilitary assistance to insurgents in El Salvador and elsewhere. The countries of Central America should be assisted in devising monitoring and verification procedures to assure that these commitments are not violated.

The other Central American nations can confront the ideological challenge of Nicaragua's Sandinista regime by meeting the needs of their own people. By making their own societies more just, equitable and prosperous, and by opening up their own political systems, the Central American countries can, in fact, test the Sandinistas through the example of their own performance.

Achieving National Reconciliation

Ending the bitter civil wars in Nicaragua, El Salvador, and Guatemala, and building the basis for national reconciliation and political opening are the most difficult tasks Central America faces. Years of deadly struggle have undermined trust and made compromise difficult in these countries. The involvement of outside powers—particularly Cuba, the Soviet Union and the United States—has deepened the region's divisions.

But the response of people throughout Central America to the Guatemala Accord—and, more recently, to the Nicaraguan cease-fire—shows the strong yearning throughout the region for an end to the fighting and for the beginning of reconciliation. *None of the parties—neither the governments nor the insurgents nor any other group in the region—can afford to ignore the vast constituency for peace.* The great contribution of the Guatemala Accord was to provide a framework to stop the region's armed conflicts and to encourage peaceful political competition. Each government in Central America is committed by the Guatemala Accord to provide constitutional guarantees for a pluralist political system in which all segments of society will be free to participate. All the region's governments have promised to hold regularly scheduled elections and to protect freedoms of assembly, association and expression. Insurgents, in turn, are urged to lay down their arms and rejoin their respective political communities.

Implementing this blueprint for peace will not be easy, as the past few months have made abundantly clear. But the Sapoá agreement between the government of Nicaragua and the Contra leadership was a major step in the right direction, and a great deal can be done in the months ahead to foster reconciliation throughout Central America.

The three Central American governments that have faced civil wars—Nicaragua, El Salvador, and Guatemala—must now convince the insurgents that laying down their arms will not amount to surrender or suicide but will open the way for participation in national affairs. As a first step, governments in the region must put an end to violence directed against their opponents. Nicaragua should permit political rallies and other peaceful opposition activities to take place, without intimidation from mob violence. El Salvador, Guatemala, and Honduras should work to stop political assassinations and "disappearances," and apprehend and punish those who commit these crimes.

Both the governments and the insurgents— in El Salvador and Guatemala as in Nicaragua—must also be prepared to negotiate and abide by effective cease-fire agreements. Such agreements should not give military advantage to either side, but should initiate a period of confidence-building that can eventually lead to a permanent cessation of hostilities. During this transition period, the insurgents must have an opportunity to test governmental pledges of democratic pluralism and constitutional guarantees.

Governments must allow their opponents to organize openly and compete freely in municipal and legislative elections, elections for the proposed Central American Parliament, and eventual presidential elections. Although elections alone cannot produce democracy, they are crucial to political opening and national reconciliation. Opposition groups in every country should use these contests to channel their efforts into peaceful political activity, and to test their popular strength. We repudiate efforts by any group to disrupt electoral processes by threatening voters, attacking polling places, or intimidating candidates and elected officials.

Central America today is still a long way from political pluralism and constitutional democracy. Abuses of human rights and interference with free political activity occur regularly in El Salvador, Guatemala, Honduras, and Nicaragua. In Nicaragua, despite the Sapoá truce, it is still far from clear whether the Sandinistas fully accept the legitimacy of autonomous political opposition. In El Salvador and Guatemala, military and police forces often act outside of civilian political control. In Honduras, both civilian and military institutions are weak and subject to corruption.

These four countries are different, but in all of them international vigilance can reinforce those who are committed to the rule of law. Countries outside Central America can contribute to reconciliation by providing technical assistance for negotiating and verifying cease-fire arrangements, by sending qualified observers to monitor elections, and by working to protect fundamental human rights. Persistent international support for freedom of expression and association throughout Central America can also help to expand political space.

Vigorous constitutional democracies will not emerge overnight in the Central American countries that have never known democracy. The genius of the Guatemala Accord, however, is its marshalling of concerted, symmetric, and reciprocal international pressures and incentives, aimed at persuading all countries of the isthmus to open their politics and allow opposition elements to operate without fear of retribution. These pressures and incentives are much more likely than armed attack—or mere exhortation—to pave the way toward national reconciliation, pluralist politics, and democracy. The incipient progress already made in Nicaragua must be bolstered; it may set an example for peace in El Salvador, where the civil war is of longer duration and probably even more intractable.

Caring for the Refugees

Two million or more Central Americans, from El Salvador, Guatemala and Nicaragua, have fled their homes during these years of strife. More than half have moved within their own countries, mostly from rural areas to crowded urban centers. The rest have sought refuge abroad: some in Honduras and Costa Rica, and many more in Mexico, the United States, and Canada.

Most of these displaced persons, whether in their own countries or elsewhere in the region, are living in extreme poverty. A minority reside in camps run by the United Nations High Commission for Refugees (UNHCR); most others are less fortunate. Jobs and social services for the refugees are scarce, but they are fearful of returning home to countries where political violence compounds economic deprivation.

So long as Central America's armed struggles continue, there can be no solution to the problems of refugees and displaced persons. But even a secure peace would not by itself solve these problems. Many displaced people cannot or will not return to their place of origin. Those who do return will encounter difficult conditions: shortages of jobs, land, housing, and public services. After years of war and economic stagnation, no Central American country can easily accommodate refugees. If the region's refugees were to return home without arrangements for their reintegration, they could disrupt the fragile peace process by further straining local economies and exacerbating political tensions.

It is vital, both for humanitarian reasons and to preserve the possibility of peace, that the governments of Central America be helped to resettle the refugees, whether or not in their countries of origin. Central America's refugees require assistance to meet basic needs: emergency food, medical care, education, housing and legal services. International agencies— including the UNHCR, the International Committee of the Red Cross (ICRC), and other groups— have already been playing a critical role; their efforts should be strengthened and generously supported by the international community. A minimum of $250 million will be needed to begin addressing the problems of Central America's displaced and refugee populations; no investment in regional security would be better spent.

Central American governments, for their part, should facilitate the work of the international agencies to help refugees, and should safeguard their rights. And they need to get on, as soon as possible, with the task of economic recovery. Central America's refugees can only be fully reintegrated when the economies of the region are revitalized and when expanded rural employment slows the flood of migrants into Central America's cities.

The United States, Canada and Mexico should suspend deportations to Central America to avoid placing an additional burden on the region. Central American refugees should, at the least, be granted safe haven in the countries where they now reside; consideration should be given to extending to them the right to legal resettlement.

One difficult problem that demands special attention is the fate of the Contras. As negotiations proceed to end Nicaragua's civil war, every effort should be made to assure that the rebel forces and their supporters can be reincorporated into Nicaragua's political and economic life. Admittedly, this will not be easy to achieve. The Contras have deep grievances against the Sandinista regime, with which they have fought bitterly. For their part, the Sandinistas will find it difficult, in practice, to welcome back the counter-revolutionary leaders. Nicaragua's economy, moreover, is devastated. Even if they faced no animosity, the Contras would have a difficult time subsisting if they all returned soon to Nicaragua.

As external support for their insurgency ends, it is likely that many of the Contras will seek refuge in Costa Rica and Honduras. If they are followed by family members and supporters, this exodus might ultimately involve as many as 100,000 people. Neither Honduras nor Costa Rica can comfortably absorb such a massive influx. It would strain their economies, create serious security and law enforcement problems, and complicate their relations with Nicaragua.

There is no easy solution for this quandary, but some steps should be taken. Nicaragua should be pressed to provide security guarantees and economic assistance to facilitate the return of those Contras willing to lay down their arms. Those Contras who wish to settle in Nicaragua should be strongly encouraged to avail themselves of the proffered amnesty. The international community should extend assistance to ease the Contras' reintegration into Nicaragua's normal life. The signatories of the Guatemala Accord, other governments of the Hemisphere, the United Nations High Commission for Refugees and the International Committee of the Red Cross should monitor the treatment of these persons and assure that their rights are fully respected.

Those among the Contras who are now ready to disarm but are not prepared to return immediately to Nicaragua should be helped to remain in Central America, with the hope that evolving conditions in Nicaragua may allow them to go back later. The United States and other countries of the Hemisphere should provide assistance to them through international relief organizations. International assistance should be especially generous for those

Central American countries that provide a home to these victims of Central America's turmoil.

For those Contra leaders who are unable or unwilling to return to Nicaragua under the Sandinistas, we urge that the United States recognize its special responsibility and offer to resettle them. It may be necessary to create a special humanitarian entry category under U.S. immigration law to admit these refugees. Federal aid to the relevant communities should help them offer resettlement assistance, job training, and language education.

Promoting Equitable Development

Almost until the outbreak of violence in the late 1970s, Central America's economies had been growing rapidly for a generation. From 1950 until 1978, the region's annual economic expansion averaged more than five percent. Real per capita income more than doubled. Central America greatly enlarged its physical infrastructure—including roads, port facilities, electric power, and mass communications. Agriculture was modernized and diversified, and foreign trade multiplied. Industrial production rose sharply. The Central American Common Market, established in 1961, provided a powerful stimulus to this impressive economic progress.

The benefits of the region's rapid growth, however, were very unevenly distributed. Income, wealth, and land were all highly concentrated. More than 40 percent of Central America's people, and more than half of its rural population, continued to live in extreme poverty. The poorest 20 percent of Central America's population shared less than four percent of the region's income. More than half of the region's children were malnourished. Except in Costa Rica, Central America's striking socioeconomic inequities were hardly diminished by the economic growth of the 1970s. In some countries, they got worse.

By 1980, Central America's economic expansion had ground to a halt. The easy initial phase of regional import substitution had been exhausted, and the limits of domestic markets imposed both by small scale and by maldistribution of income became more evident. Agricultural and industrial production slowed, unemployment and underemployment mounted, export earnings declined, and interest payments on the region's foreign debt soared. Except for Guatemala, which has its own petroleum, the energy-poor countries of Central America were also jarred by the oil price shocks of the 1970s.

This economic downturn has persisted through the 1980s, exacerbated by a deadly combination of internal political violence, world recession, and natural catastrophes. Central America's economies have suffered from outright physical destruction, the burden of refugees, the loss of investor confidence, and the dislocation caused by military expenditures.

Per capita income for Central America as a whole has fallen almost 25 percent during the past decade—even more in Nicaragua and El Salvador, where the fighting has been concentrated. Nicaragua's economy is near collapse, with inflation now over 1,000 percent per year, prices grossly distorted, and basic goods in short supply. El Salvador's economic deterioration has been cushioned by massive U.S. economic and military assistance, totalling over $3.5 billion since 1981. Costa Rica and Honduras, too, have become increasingly dependent on U.S. aid.

Central America's economies will not recover as long as they are burdened by continuing wars or the likelihood of their resumption. But even when peace is finally achieved, economic vitality will not quickly be restored. It will take time—and major infusions of international aid—to reconstruct what has been destroyed.

And peace is unlikely to endure long unless Central America is able to promote social and economic development that is more equitable than that of the past. Central America must break its tragic cycle of deprivation, unrest, repression, and revolt. The governments of the region should improve education and health services and make special efforts to involve the poor, including women, more fully and productively in the region's growth. Agrarian reforms and other redistributive measures are needed to open the way toward generating employment and income for the disadvantaged. As Central America's presidents have affirmed together, peace and democracy cannot be achieved without development.

Even during the current period, in which war and peace are in uncertain balance, it is urgent to ease the plight of the victims of war, including both the hundreds of thousands of refugees and those who are suffering in their own communities. Emergency programs must be put into place to relieve hunger, improve health care, and provide decent housing.

Beyond these immediate needs, the international community must stand ready to help Central America reactivate its economies and start to alleviate mass poverty. External assistance should be provided to improve social services, rebuild infrastructure, and expand the region's productive base. *The United States alone has spent some $6 billion in Central America during the 1980s, much of it for military purposes. At least as much should be devoted in the next five years to help reconstruct the region's economies.*

Now is the time to begin planning for Central America's future. We endorse the efforts of public and private organizations— including those of the United Nations Economic Commission for Latin America and the Caribbean, the European Economic Community, and the International Commission on Central American Recovery and Development— to design concrete proposals for regional development.

Priority attention should be given to Central America's critical problems of debt and trade. During the next five years at least, industrial country creditors should allocate interest payments on Central America's official bilateral debt to a special fund for the whole region's reconstruction. The industrial nations should also offer improved access to their markets for Central America's principal exports and offer compensatory financing to Central America when export prices drop. To the extent possible, the international community should seek to promote regional approaches to Central America's development, and to help rebuild the Central American Common Market. Regional measures often make the most sense economically and they could reinforce the peace process.

Ultimately, peace, security, development and democracy are all indivisible in Central America. Social and economic inequities and pervasive repression have fueled the region's insurgencies. The wars, in turn, have blocked economic progress and intensified the repression. It will be difficult to build democratic politics in fractured societies torn by violence, but Central America cannot achieve lasting peace unless all major social and political groups feel they can participate in shaping the region's future.

Only the Central Americans themselves can build a better future. Against formidable odds, they have taken many important steps and accomplished much in recent months. Although setbacks will surely occur, Central America is moving forward.

Now that the people and governments of Central America have pointed the way, it is time for the rest of us in the Americas strongly to support their efforts. External financial assistance will clearly be needed to care for the refugees, to reconstruct the region's economies, and to lay the foundations for equitable and democratic development. All countries of the Hemisphere must also show patience, understanding, and restraint in their relations with Central America. These are precisely the qualities that make democracy possible wherever it exists. After years of violence, the people of Central America deserve to achieve their shared vision of peace.

Chapter II

The Debt Trap: Still No Escape

For six years, Latin America has been mired in debt and depression. The costs of this region-wide crisis are mounting both for Latin America and its creditors. Yet there is still no firm consensus on how to resolve Latin America's debt problems and revive its damaged economies.

The creditors— commercial banks, international financial institutions, and the governments of the industrialized countries— mostly remain committed to the strategy for managing international debt advanced by U.S. Treasury Secretary James Baker in September 1985. The Baker proposals for restoring economic growth in Latin America and elsewhere in the Third World call for a combination of economic reforms in the debtor countries and new public and private lending to meet their capital needs.

Latin American governments, however, have lost confidence in the Baker approach, for it has not produced the resources it promised. Few knowledgeable Latin Americans expect that it ever will. Many now see debt relief— to reduce the region's financial obligations and massive capital outflows— as the only way for Latin America to escape its economic bind.

These contrasting perspectives may well produce increasing confrontation between debtors and creditors in the next months or years. In many countries of Latin America and the Caribbean, the political forces calling for suspension or even repudiation of debt payments are already gaining ground, while moderate and pragmatic leaders searching for cooperative approaches are on the defensive. With presidential elections scheduled throughout much of Latin America in the next two years, pressures will intensify to ease austerity and curtail interest payments in order to promote short-term economic expansion. Conflicts between the Latin American debtors and their creditors will become harder to avoid.

Confrontation, however, is not inevitable. The past six years of economic distress have taught both debtors and creditors some basic truths, on which a common strategy could and should be built. A cooperative inter-American approach to debt management can still be constructed, based on three key points.

First, sustained growth must be the centerpiece of any solution to Latin America's debt problems. The countries of the region can only achieve that growth if they undertake extensive policy reforms and have access to adequate financial resources.

Second, unilateral actions carry a high price. Most Latin American countries are trying hard to meet their debt obligations. Brazil's recent accord with its commercial creditors, ending the country's year-long suspension of interest payments, underscored the importance for debtor countries of normal relations with the international financial community—and the high costs of disrupting those relations.

Third, failing to act decisively now entails serious long-term risks for all parties: postponed development, increased social tensions, and political instability in Latin America; reduced exports and weakened financial systems in the United States and other industrialized countries; growing losses and continuing risk for private banks worldwide; and declining credibility for international financial organizations. Prolonged economic adversity could destroy the best chance ever for building a community of democratic nations in the Americas.

A Lost Decade
Latin America's economic downturn began in 1982, when three decades of uninterrupted growth came to an end. Interest payments on the region's past loans soared, export earnings plummeted in the wake of world recession, and commercial credit dried up. Nearly every Latin American economy went into a tailspin in 1982 and 1983. After four straight years of slow growth, beginning in 1984,

the region's per capita income is still some eight percent below its 1980 level. Only two countries—Brazil and Colombia—have restored incomes to their pre-crisis levels, while many have seen the gains of one and even two full decades wiped out. A few countries, most notably Colombia, have made strides toward recovery. But most remain in deep economic slumps, with growth proceeding by fits and starts. Inflation and high unemployment are rampant.

Latin America's debt obligations frustrate recovery in several ways. Most obviously, they drain away resources. In the past five years, Latin America has paid out upwards of $120 billion more in principal and interest than it has obtained in new loans. This outflow has absorbed more than four percent of the region's gross national product and 20 percent of its export earnings, forcing sharp cutbacks in imports vital for production. Only a portion of these imports have been replaced by expanding domestic industry.

Debt payments, combined with an unfavorable business climate, also deprive Latin America of capital desperately needed for investment. The region today is investing some 25 percent less than it was in 1980. In many countries, machinery, plants, and infrastructure are depreciating faster than they are being replaced. Growth is imperiled for years to come.

Interest payments—both domestic and international— place a heavy strain on government budgets, contributing to large fiscal deficits and inflationary pressures. Inflation is a hidden tax through which governments obtain the immense resources required to service their debts. The private sector is thus depleted of the capital it requires for growth and investment. The burden ultimately falls most heavily on the poor, particularly women and children.

The social consequences of Latin America's prolonged depression are multiplying. The people of Latin America have seen their wages fall and their jobs disappear; their housing, schools, hospitals, and other public services have deteriorated; and they have endured food shortages and mounting street crime. Financially-strapped governments have not been able to address such fundamental social problems as the vast gap between rich and poor, the deep poverty of rural areas and city slums, widespread malnutrition and high rates of infant mortality. And these problems are getting worse. They are tearing at the political and social fabric of much of Latin America, and could yet reverse the region's recent turn toward democracy.

Latin America's financial plight has also affected the world's industrial countries—none more than the United States. U.S. exports to Latin America have sharply decreased in the 1980s. Because of the debt crisis, Latin America buys some $20 to $30 billion per year less from the United States than it would if the region's growth had not been interrupted. Latin America's debt makes it harder to resolve the U.S. trade deficit, and lost trade has meant lost jobs for hundreds of thousands of workers in the United States. Investment opportunities in Latin America for U.S. corporations have also diminished. Annual U.S. investment in the region is currently 25 percent of pre-1982 levels.

Latin America's economic distress affects the United States in other ways as well. Pressure for migration to the United States is far greater today because so many Latin Americans are losing faith in their own economies. The hemispheric drug trade is more difficult to control because Latin America cannot provide alternatives to the jobs and income now derived from narcotics.

To the extent that economic failure imperils the future of democracy in the Americas, it also endangers hemispheric security. The security of the Americas is best protected by strong democratic governments sharing basic social and civic values. These governments are the most reliable defense against the expansion of guerrilla activity or the intrusion of Soviet power in the Americas.

Debt Management is Becoming More Difficult

It has been getting harder for Latin America to deal with its debt burden. Overall debt obligations have grown from $330 billion at the outset of the crisis in 1982 to approximately $420 billion in 1988. In 1981, Latin America's debt obligations amounted to two and one half times the value of the region's annual exports; in 1988, they are nearly four times greater than exports. The most important indicator of Latin America's debt management capacity, the ratio of its debt service payments to export earnings, has improved little over the past five years, despite a steep drop in international interest rates.

By 1986, eight Latin American countries— Bolivia, Costa Rica, Cuba, the Dominican Republic, Ecuador, Honduras, Nicaragua, and Peru—had stopped paying interest on their commercial debt. Brazil, the region's largest debtor, joined that group in February 1987.

Brazil's suspension of interest payments was particularly significant. Not only was its commercial debt of some $110 billion more than three times that of all other non-paying countries combined, but its economic performance had been the region's strongest since the emergence of the debt crisis. Until Brazilian authorities allowed economic expansion to proceed unchecked for too long, Brazil was earning enough from exports to pay its interest bills and still grow by a hefty seven percent per year—all without new loans. Many analysts pointed to Brazil as proof that countries could both grow out of the debt trap and meet their external obligations, if only they pursued the right policies. It was poor economic management that caused Brazil's sharp reversal, but the impact was multiplied by the country's enormous debt—to the point of economic and political crisis.

The Disappointing Results of the Baker Plan

The strategy guiding debt management since 1982, in sum, has been only partially successful. It has avoided widespread defaults that might have threatened the solvency and stability of banking systems worldwide, but it has not done much to alleviate the problems of the debtor countries. The strategy had counted on a combination of new public and private lending, economic reform in Latin America, and improvements in the world economy to defuse the debt crisis—and to rekindle growth in Latin America and restore the region's access to commercial credit. But regional recovery has been slow and spotty, and there is no sign that voluntary commercial lending will be resumed any time soon.

The 1985 Baker proposals, designed to reinforce the prevailing strategy, have so far produced few concrete results. Instead of expanding their commitments to Latin America, as Baker proposed, commercial banks have reduced them. In 1986, the banks collected almost as much in principal as they disbursed in new credit. Less than five percent of the region's commercial interest bill of nearly $30 billion was offset by private bank loans. Substantial loans made to Mexico and Argentina accounted for most of the aggregate increase in bank lending to the region in 1987. Few other countries obtained much commercial financing, except for short-term trade credits.

Treasury Secretary Baker, among others, has encouraged commercial banks to consider a wider range (or "menu") of financing options to increase capital flows to Latin America. So far, however, the menu approach has produced few additional resources. Although banks may make more extensive use of the new financial instruments as these become more familiar, this has not happened yet.

Commercial banks will continue to reschedule loans to defer repayment of principal and will remain a critical source of trade credits. But more substantial financing from private lenders, much beyond the modest amounts they are now providing, do not now appear likely. The decision of major U.S. banks in mid-1987 to set aside large reserves against their Third World loans confirmed the high risks they assigned to this debt. It was a clear signal that the banks intended to keep future lending to a minimum.

Banks operate on small profit margins, and are already absorbing large losses on their Latin American loans. Many countries are accumulating interest arrears; few are repaying any principal at all; and interest rates are barely in excess of what banks pay for new money. The banks know how financially troubled Latin America is, and they want to avoid even larger losses. They have safer and more profitable ways to invest. Commercial credit will likely follow, not lead, recovery in Latin America. The outlook for official financing—from the World Bank, the International Monetary Fund (IMF), and the Inter-American Development Bank (IDB)—is mixed. In the past two years, the World Bank boosted its lending to Latin America, but it also collected more principal and interest, so the net amount of resources transferred grew only modestly. The IMF and IDB provided even less capital than previously. In 1986 and 1987, the IMF collected more in debt service than it made available in new loans. A projected expansion of IDB financing has been stalled by a dispute between the United States and the Latin American countries over control of the Bank's operations.

The United States and the other industrialized countries have recently agreed to expand substantially the World Bank's lending capacity. But the U.S. contribution, on which the arrangement depends, hinges on uncertain Congressional approval.

The IMF is studying programs to help protect debtor nations from sudden surges in interest rates or declines in export prices. If they materialize, these long-overdue measures will help to buffer the region against sharp changes in the international economy, but they will not provide much added capital for Latin America. The United States and the other industrialized countries control the policies and lending capacities of the international financial organizations. These institutions cannot play a significant role in international debt management unless their major donors provide the necessary support. It is urgent that the dispute affecting the Inter-American Development Bank be resolved, and that full support be provided for its expansion.

The Stagnating International Economy

The troubled world economy of the 1980s has severely hampered Latin America's economic recovery. Growth has been substantially slower than in the 1960s and 1970s—and less than the three percent widely considered the minimum needed for Latin America to trade its way out of the debt crisis.

The demand and prices for Latin America's exports have been depressed for most of the decade. While the volume of those exports has risen by 30 percent since 1980, earnings have not kept pace, as average prices dropped by about 25 percent during the same period. Although they have improved recently, the prices of Latin America's principal exports have been at historically low levels for much of the 1980s. Erratic petroleum prices have particularly affected the region's oil exporting countries. The most encouraging development in the world economy has been the sharp decline (of about 50 percent) in interest rates since 1984, but those rates are now creeping upwards once again.

If world trade and economic growth regain their dynamism— and if interest rates hold steady— Latin America's economic prospects would be certainly brighter. Conversely, a major downturn in the world economy, particularly one accompanied by higher interest rates, would push the region as a whole more deeply into depression. Latin America remains highly vulnerable to international economic trends beyond its control.

What happens in the U.S. economy is especially important. The United States is Latin America's largest trading partner, and continuing U.S. economic expansion has kept world growth from slipping further. But the prospects for the U.S. economy over the next few years are uncertain. A slowdown, if not a recession, now appears likely as trade and fiscal deficits threaten to erode domestic and international confidence in the U.S. economy. If this drop in confidence were to accelerate flight from the dollar and push U.S. interest rates higher, Latin America's economies would be squeezed by rising interest bills and lower export earnings. For most countries, debt would become much harder to manage.

The best way to avoid this chain of events is for Washington to deal sensibly and soon with its trade and fiscal problems. But other industrial nations must do their share as well. The trade surplus countries of Europe and Asia, particularly West Germany and Japan, must stimulate domestic growth and open their markets wider to pick up any slack produced by a contracting U.S. economy. Even so, world growth cannot be counted on as a major stimulus to growth and trade expansion in Latin America.

Policy and Politics in Latin America

In varying degrees, Latin American countries have

improved their economic management. Trade policy reforms, particularly the setting of realistic exchange rates, have led to expanded exports. Higher interest rates have reduced capital flight from many countries, and in several places, some repatriation of capital has occurred. Only a few countries, however, have progressed very far in other areas. In virtually every Latin American country, government bureaucracies and public enterprises remain bloated and inefficient, and the state retains far too large a role in most economies. Governments have not done much to turn state firms over to private management. In several places, legislation has made foreign ownership easier, but the changes have been too modest to attract many outside investors.

Fundamental economic reform is never easy to accomplish. Shortages of foreign capital and cramped domestic budgets make reform even more difficult in Latin America today. Public and private enterprises, for example, lack the resources needed to exploit new export opportunities.

Politics also stymie necessary policy changes. Large segments of the population often feel the costs of such changes right away. The benefits typically take much longer to realize. Many countries have initiated tough measures to control fiscal deficits and inflation, but could not sustain them over time. Brazil and Argentina launched innovative anti-inflation campaigns in 1986 and 1987. After showing encouraging early results, both subsequently collapsed, underscoring the difficulty of fiscal reform in weak economies where the public demands quick improvement.

Latin America's stop-and-go performance has eroded the confidence of business and financial communities throughout the region. There is little willingness in any sector to accept further sacrifices. Few Latin Americans still believe that such sacrifices will produce significant and lasting results.

Many Latin Americans now oppose market-oriented policies because they associate such policies with austerity, unemployment, and reduced social expenditures. Organized labor actively resists reforms that threaten to eliminate jobs and lower wages. Other resistance comes from owners of businesses, anxious to preserve protected markets and state subsidies, and from public employees, concerned about their jobs and influence. Governments pursuing market approaches risk losing support to more populist opponents. *Domestic politics are also making it harder for many Latin American governments to reach accommodation with their creditors.* The prospects are for more, not less, confrontation. When eight Latin American presidents—including the leaders of the region's five largest debtors—met in Acapulco in November 1987, the debt crisis dominated the agenda. They stressed the growing economic hardships and political difficulties of debt servicing, and repeatedly emphasized that economic failure was jeopardizing progress toward democracy. Although they stopped short of any concerted action, the presidents urged that debt service be reduced to each country's ability to pay. That ability is not a question of economics alone but also of political choice.

Alternative Solutions

Two contrasting approaches to debt management compete for adherents in 1988. One is the strategy now in place—essentially the 1985 Baker plan, enhanced by the new "menu" of financing options. This approach, in effect one of "muddling through," emphasizes the need for more sweeping economic reforms in Latin America. It calls for the full and timely payment of interest, although recognizing that principal will remain unpaid. The region's capital needs are to be met on a case-by-case basis, largely through new public and private lending.

The alternative approach—concessional debt relief—also requires improved economic management in Latin America. Rather than depend mainly on additional lending to satisfy Latin America's capital requirements, however, this approach relies on a significant reduction of debt obligations to stem the flow of resources out of the region.

Fortifying the Baker Approach

Advocates of the Baker strategy, including some members of the Dialogue, foresee a gradual strengthening of Latin America's economies as policy reforms take hold, countries expand their exports, and the flow of external financing picks up. Overall debt will increase in the short-run—but the burden of that debt, relative to exports and production, should begin to diminish as recovery proceeds.

The Baker plan, according to its proponents, has already produced important progress toward its twin objectives of satisfactory growth and improved creditworthiness in Latin America. They point to the economic reforms introduced in many countries, to improving interest-to-export ratios, and to Latin America's four straight years of per capita growth. They are optimistic about the prospects of additional financing from the commercial banks, with their stronger capital positions and expanded reserves against losses, and from the major international financial institutions. Even those who advocate this approach, however, recognize its weaknesses:

- Some Latin American countries are so overloaded with debt and have such poorly performing economies that they will never be able to pay their interest bills. These countries have already accumulated large arrears. Private banks have taken no legal actions against them, but neither have they been willing to forgive these loans, for they fear to establish a precedent for other debtor nations which might demand similar treatment. By now, however, the economic prospects of these countries are so bleak that most of their debt should probably be explicitly forgiven. This has essentially been done for Bolivia, which is using new loans to repurchase its debt at a small fraction of its face value. Debt forgiveness would help alleviate the uncertainty and disorder of the weakest debtors' international financial relationships, and would establish a sounder basis for their economic management. The costs to their creditors would be small since the countries in greatest need of such relief account for less than 15 percent of all Latin American debt—and most of them have already stopped paying, in any case.

- Because of their weak balance of payments position, the countries of Latin America are extremely vulnerable to external "shocks." A surge in interest rates or a further decline in export prices would throw many of the region's economies into disarray—as the sharp drop in oil prices did to Mexico in 1986. The proposed IMF programs to assist countries through such shocks would help. Contingency financing to protect countries against sudden changes in the world economy might also be incorporated as a standard feature of new loan packages—as did Mexico's 1987 package which promised increased lending if oil prices dropped beneath a certain level. A cap on interest rates would provide still greater protection. Interest obligations resulting from a rise in rates beyond the cap would not be collected; they would instead be added to the value of existing loans, i.e., "capitalized."

- *The greatest weakness of "muddling through" is the uncertainty about whether sufficient new financing will, in fact, be made available to Latin America.* Although the flow from public and private sources has been unsatisfactory for the past several years, there are some reasons to be encouraged. The proposed $75 billion addition to the World Bank's capital, if it is approved, will allow for significantly greater lending. If the United States and Latin American countries can resolve their dispute, the Inter-American Development Bank will have resources to double its lending. In addition to standard balance of payments loans, commercial banks now have an extensive "menu" of financing alternatives from which to choose. Latin America's financial situation and its prospects for recovery would improve if these initiatives were implemented. The Baker approach would best be fortified by providing the debtor countries with solid assurances of adequate external financing. A first step would be to fix, for each Latin American country, a multi-year target for external financing. Such targets would be part of an overall economic plan for the country that would also set agreed-upon goals for policy reform. The idea is to create realistic and mutually-reinforcing performance objectives for both creditors and debtors, which might then be monitored by the IMF and the World Bank. If a country fails to adhere to its reform commitments, according to this approach, that country would lose access to its claim on new credits. Likewise, if creditors fail to come up with the target financing, most Dialogue members would allow the country to defer interest payments to make up the difference, provided that sound economic policies are being followed.

The Baker strategy, as it stands, clearly has deficiencies, but the parties involved, particularly the industrialized country governments, could take measures to remedy many of them. *Since the Baker approach remains official policy, it is urgent now that every effort be made to improve its chances of success; that is, to assure that Latin America has adequate financing and appropriate incentives to pursue sensible policies.*

Debt Relief

Throughout Latin America—and increasingly in some circles in the industrialized countries—there is widespread skepticism that the region's economic problems can be solved by muddling through. A majority of Dialogue members share that skepticism, and are ready to endorse a more comprehensive approach to the debt crisis, one that includes substantial debt relief for every Latin American country. Most of us believe that debt levels throughout the region are already too high—and that they must now be reduced, not further increased, as the Baker approach requires. Indeed, many Dialogue participants are persuaded that extensive debt relief has become virtually inevitable—given current political and economic trends in Latin America, the uncertain world economy, and the continued slow pace of commercial lending. *The central question, for many of us, is not whether debt relief is justified and necessary, but how to bring it about in the most constructive and orderly way.*

From the outset of the debt crisis in 1982, a great variety of proposals for reducing Latin America's debt burden have been put forth. Recently, as Latin American loans have been selling at increasing discounts in secondary markets, most attention has focused on formulas that allow the debtor countries to obtain the benefits of those discounts. Although the precise mechanisms of each formula vary, they generally call for some agency— the World Bank, a specially-created facility, or industrial country governments— to repurchase commercial loans at their deflated market values. Each country's obligations would then be reduced by the difference between the face and market value of its repurchased loans.

Commercial creditors would take most of the losses involved (aside from that passed on to the governments because of reduced tax liabilities). They would, however, receive secure and marketable assets in exchange— and they would no longer be called upon to join in new lending packages for Latin America. Participating banks would be able to clear their portfolios of high risk Latin American loans.

The benefits of debt-repurchase schemes to Latin America depend on the amount of the debt that is swapped, on the discount offered, and on the portion of the discount that is transferred to the debtor countries. Most such schemes focus on the approximately $250 billion in medium- and long-term loans that are held by commercial banks and owed or guaranteed by governments. These loans account for some 60 percent of the region's overall debt. The remaining 40 percent is largely official loans from international financial institutions and short-term trade credits. For most countries, new lending in these categories is expected to exceed repayment obligations so relief is not necessary.

With market discounts now averaging about 50 cents on the dollar, exchanging all of Latin America's medium- to long-term commercial loans would erase some $125 billion of the region's debt. The annual $10 billion interest savings would far exceed the amount of new commercial lending that is now anticipated. The region would still need roughly another $10 billion in external financing to achieve satisfactory growth of five percent per year. International financial institutions would have to expand their lending to provide this additional financing, the exact amount of which would have to be calculated on a country-by-country basis.

All of us recognize that debt relief poses many serious problems:

First, commercial banks would immediately face such large losses that the solvency of some of them would be threatened. This is not an issue for most Japanese and European banks, or for U.S. regional banks; all these banks together hold 75 to 80 percent of Latin America's commercial debt. They can accommodate the losses because they either hold a limited amount of Latin American loans or have built significant reserves against those loans. Several major U.S. banks, however, would have to cut deeply into equity capital in order to write-off half of their Latin American debt. They would be severely weakened—unless they obtained U.S. Treasury support or at least regulatory changes that would allow them to absorb the losses over ten or more years. Each bank would have to make its own calculations on whether to participate in a debt relief program—and decide what share of its loans to swap. A successful debt relief operation does not require the full participation of every commercial bank. But the more banks that take part, the greater the interest savings to Latin America's debtors.

Few banks chose to participate in the recent Mexico debt repurchase plan—and the amount of relief obtained was far below initial expectations. But in that case the banks were asked to exchange their loans for Mexican bonds, on which only the principal, and not the interest, was guaranteed. Banks would have been more willing to take part if, in exchange for their debt holdings, they had been offered fully assured assets. This, however, would have required financial support from the United States or other industrialized countries.

Second, so far neither United States, Japan, nor the countries of Western Europe have shown any willingness to provide resources to finance an extensive debt relief program. These countries, particularly the United States, have been slow even to endorse new funding for the international financial institutions, which requires far smaller outlays than would a major debt relief operation.

There is not much political support yet in the industrialized countries for making resources available to reduce Third World debt.

Governments would have to come up with sizable resources—but the amounts are not impossible. It would take a reserve of some $15 to $20 billion for the World Bank or a new agency to issue bonds with which to repurchase $250 billion of Latin America's commercial debt at current market discounts. This is not a small sum, but it is less than the combined annual debt service payments of Brazil and Mexico.

Most of us believe that the current official opposition to debt relief is ill-advised. The costs to the industrialized countries would be significant, but substantial gains would be achieved from restoring Latin America's economic vitality, expanding the region's trade, and strengthening banking systems worldwide.

Third, debt relief benefits most those Latin American countries whose debt sells at the largest discount—and the weaker a country's economic performance and debt repayment record, the greater the discount is likely to be. Among the largest beneficiaries would be those countries that have followed the worst policies and have been least responsible in meeting their payment obligations. The promise of debt relief, moreover, offers a perverse incentive for governments to adopt policies that would further depress the market value of their loans. That incentive can be attenuated by negotiating the amount of relief each country receives, rather than simply transferring the full savings of the market discount—but such negotiations would clearly add to the operational difficulties of any debt relief program.

It is critical that any debt relief initiative provide positive inducements for countries to adopt desirable policy changes. No country's debt, for example, should be exchanged until that country gains World Bank and IMF approval for a multi-year development plan incorporating structural and policy reforms. These international financial institutions must condition any further lending to the country on the implementation of the approved economic plan.

Finally, debt relief may harm longer-term growth prospects by damaging the credit standing of Latin American countries for years to come, thereby cutting them off from essential financing as their economies recover. It may be possible to avoid this danger if debt relief is not imposed on the creditor banks, but rather is voluntary and mutually agreed-upon, and if countries carry out their side of the bargain by pursuing sound policies. The countries might even become more creditworthy over time if debt relief succeeds in restoring growth and business confidence. But there is no getting around the fact that, at least for a time, foreign banks experiencing major losses on loans to a country will be less inclined to lend to that country. Debt relief certainly has that cost.

Seeking Consensus

Although members of the Dialogue do not all agree on the best formula to address Latin America's economic and financial problems, all of us know that Latin America must have access to more resources if it is to recover from its current financial plight and achieve adequate growth into the future. *Most of us favor a major program of debt relief, combined with stepped-up lending from international financial institutions. Some believe, however, that debt relief is impractical and would ultimately be harmful to the common objectives we all share.*

Despite these differences, we all agree on eight fundamental points:

● Latin America's problems are already very serious. If not effectively addressed, they will grow worse, with grave consequences for the entire Hemisphere. It is urgent to restore economic growth to Latin America as quickly as possible. That growth must be sufficiently vigorous— at least five percent per year for the region as a whole— to avoid political disaffection and renew public confidence in democratic governments. It must permit higher wages and more jobs, the alleviation of absolute poverty, and steady progress toward social justice.

- Not enough is being done to address Latin America's debt problems. Concerted action by all major parties is needed now to avoid the damage of unilateral initiatives. If either the Latin American countries or their creditors try to go it alone, that will only aggravate the problems and prolong the region's economic agony.

- Every country of Latin America must adopt sound economic policies. Each country should formulate a comprehensive multi-year development program that sets out targets and schedules for necessary reforms in all areas of the economy, including, for example, trade, investment, taxation, financial markets, and public sector management.

- The international financial institutions must sharply accelerate their lending to Latin America. The proposed expansion of World Bank capital should be approved quickly by member countries. The United States and the nations of Latin America should end their dispute over voting procedures at the IDB, agree on the substantive reforms that should be implemented, and proceed to replenish the Bank's capital to shore up its lending capacity. The IMF must fully exploit its resources to expand credits to the region; it surely should be lending more than it is collecting in interest and principal. In addition, the U.S. Export-Import Bank and other official export credit agencies should decisively increase their support.

- Commercial banks and official creditors should now grant explicit debt relief to Latin America's weakest performing economies, most of which will never be able to pay their current obligations. The precise amount of debt to be forgiven and the formula for doing so should be negotiated between each of the countries and its creditors.

- For those countries not granted major debt relief, commercial banks should be called on to provide substantially more capital—both by expanding their lending and making far greater use of the "menu" of options now available—and to do so more expeditiously. Negotiations between the banks and the countries over new money packages have become too clumsy and drawn-out. These negotiations must be streamlined.

- Creditors and debtors should jointly establish specific targets for each country's external financing needs, sufficient to ensure an annual growth rate of five percent. These targets should be projected at least three years forward and regularly revised to take account of changes in interest rates and export prices. The creditor institutions and governments must make sure the financial targets are met for all countries that adhere to agreed-upon programs of economic reform. If a country faces a persistent shortfall in new financing, it should be allowed to defer interest payments to cover the difference.

- Finally, if all these steps do not provide enough financing needed to revive Latin America's economies, concessional debt relief may well be necessary for an increasing number of countries. Latin America cannot be allowed to endure another lost decade.

If Latin America does not escape from the debt trap soon, we foresee a growing danger that the region's governments may turn away from cooperative approaches toward unilateral actions to try to deal with their economic problems. More of them would suspend interest payments—and would, in turn, lose access to normal channels of trade credit and possibly official financing. Commercial banks would face eroding assets and mounting losses. The United States and other industrial countries would forfeit opportunities for expanded trade and investment in the region. The Latin American economies would be crippled for many years to come, social and political turmoil would surely worsen, and democratic governments would be at risk. Resolving the debt crisis remains this Hemisphere's greatest challenge.

Chapter III

Drugs: A Shared Tragedy

The use and abuse of illegal narcotics in the Hemisphere has reached staggering proportions. According to the 1987 National High School Senior Survey in the United States, 50 percent of seniors had experimented with illicit drugs, and nearly a third had tried one other than marijuana. Although some recent evidence suggests the cocaine epidemic in the United States may have peaked, consumption is now widespread and the allure of its most virulent form, "crack," continues to surge. Marijuana ranks second only to corn as a cash crop in the United States.

Illicit drug use is not a problem only for the United States. Throughout much of Latin America and the Caribbean the use of narcotics has been rising rapidly in recent years. Colombia, for example, may have more cocaine addicts per capita than the United States.

The "narcotics problem" is in fact two clusters of problems. The first is the social damage caused by drug abuse, which is intertwined with the ills that trouble all the countries of the Americas—poverty, crime, poor schools and the erosion of authority. The second is the crime and corruption that result because drugs are illegal, and so there are huge profits to be made in their illicit trafficking. The U.S. Presidential Commission on Organized Crime estimates narcotics sales to total more than $100 billion dollars in the United States, or twice what the United States spends on oil

When narco-dollars buy police, courts and elected officials, the foundations of democratic rule are shaken. In the struggling democracies of Latin America, when police are offered many times their annual salary to ignore drug dealings, or when honest judges risk death for presiding over drug cases, the threat to representative government is particularly serious.

Neither set of problems can be magically solved. No "war on drugs" will produce major victories soon, and proclamations to that effect are suspect. A better understanding of the narcotics problem, however, can help the United States and Latin America frame a more realistic, cooperative approach to their shared problem.

That approach would focus on cutting into the *demand* for drugs in the United States. It is demand that drives production and the trafficking chains criss-crossing Latin America and the Caribbean; more than a dozen countries are involved in cultivating illicit crops, in manufacturing and refining drugs, or in "downstream" operations such as smuggling or money laundering. *Until the United States curbs its demand for narcotics, traffickers will always be one step ahead of supply-side policies, leaving governments of the Hemisphere pursuing a will-of-the-wisp.*

Where We Stand in the United States

The U.S. public is worried about the drug problem: in a 1986 Chicago Council on Foreign Relations poll that asked respondents nationwide to name two or three issues of greatest concern, 26 percent cited drugs, compared with 27 percent for unemployment and just seven percent for U.S. relations with the Soviet Union. Yet attention to the issue has waxed and waned. In 1986, after a cocaine overdose killed basketball star Len Bias, public outrage peaked, and Congress quickly passed the Anti-Drug Abuse Act of 1986, an impressive declaration of intent to try to cut into the huge U.S. demand for illicit drugs. Cocaine seemed to be losing its image from the 1970s as a clean, safe, even glamorous drug—the choice of rock stars, athletes and actors.

Yet since this burst of indignation, the U.S. Administration has cut back funding for efforts to curb the demand for drugs. Although ritual denunciations of drug abuse as the ruination of young people continue, politicians have moved on to other issues. In the words of a <u>New York Times</u>

editorial, it is not that the United States lost the war on drugs, it is rather that "we never really decided to get into it."

Behind this seesawing public attention, it is plain that efforts to restrict the supply of drugs in the United States are failing. From 1981 to 1987, federal support for drug enforcement tripled to nearly $3 billion. Even more was spent by local law enforcement agencies, an estimated $5 billion. While highly-publicized campaigns to interdict drug shipments— such as the South Florida Task Force— rack up record seizures, drugs are more plentiful in the United States than ever. Indeed, cocaine prices in the United States are dropping. A gram of cocaine sold for $600 four years ago; now the price is less than $200. And although two of the kingpins of the Colombian cocaine cartel were jailed last year, one of them even extradited to the United States, the cartel seems unaffected. No matter how many traffickers are arrested, they are easily replaced, lured in by the huge money to be made. As arrests and seizures go up, so do the amount and purity of the cocaine in the United States. Only its price falls.

The U.S. State Department's 1986 global report on narcotics put it starkly: coca production still "vastly exceeds cocaine consumption." The gap is more striking still in the case of heroin: the United States consumes only three to four percent of the approximately 2,500 tons of opium produced annually around the world. Thus, a few square miles of opium poppies can supply the entire U.S. heroin demand. As President Reagan conceded at the peak of the drug scare: "All the confiscation and law enforcement in the world will not cure this plague."

Efforts to eradicate drug crops by burning, uprooting or spraying have fared no better. Within the United States, marijuana has become the second largest cash crop, even though ten times more marijuana acreage was destroyed in 1986 than in 1984. Worse, domestic marijuana is up to ten times more potent than the Mexican product that dominated the U.S. market two decades ago. What is true of domestic eradication also holds for similar operations in Latin America. In 1986 Operation Blast Furnace, a massive ten-week, U.S.-organized effort in Bolivia, left

U.S. drug supplies and prices virtually untouched. Traffickers had stockpiled more than enough cocaine to maintain a steady flow to market.

The focus of policy must shift toward demand, but it would be foolhardy to expect dramatic results soon. In 1985, one in ten Americans were users of marijuana; by comparison, three in ten used cigarettes and six in ten alcohol. The special concern now is cocaine, and especially "crack," the potent and cheap form that is smoked. Heroin remains a tragedy of inner cities in the United States, but the number of addicts has remained constant for a decade at about a half million.

It is cocaine that has become the drug most responsible for filling U.S. hospital emergency rooms, with 25,000 cases and 1,000 deaths reported in 1986. Moreover, cocaine apparently has its own distinctive demographics. Other drugs are used predominately by 18 to 24 year-olds, but cocaine is mainly consumed by their elders.

Until last year, cocaine also was the exception to the general trend of decreasing drug use by adolescents in the 1980s. The respected annual survey by the University of Michigan shows, for instance, that daily marijuana use among high school seniors fell from its peak of 11 percent in 1978 to less than four percent in 1987. Cocaine use may have decreased for the first time in 1987. The 1987 survey found that 15 percent of high school seniors had tried it, ten percent had used it in the previous year and four percent in the previous month. For 1986 the figures were, respectively, 17, 13 and six percent.

Crack use is, however, still on the rise. The percentage of high school seniors who smoked cocaine remained constant between 1979 and 1983; between 1983 and 1986 it shot up, from 2.5 percent to six percent, due mainly to crack. Another disturbing piece of survey evidence: although the use of other drugs, such as marijuana, has declined as more people have perceived them as dangerous, that is not so for cocaine. Consumption of it so far has increased along with the public perception of its danger.

Where We Stand in Latin America

Latin American narcotics-producing countries seem to

be losing ground—if not faith—in their struggle against drugs. Despite extensive eradication efforts, the world's supply of coca leaf is estimated to have doubled in four years, with cultivation spreading from Peru and Bolivia into Colombia, Ecuador, Venezuela, Paraguay and Brazil. World cocaine production is thought to be four times U.S. demand, providing both supplies and incentives for export to Europe—and sales in Latin America. The U.S. State Department, reporting on the drug trade in 1986, concluded that:

> "Worldwide production of illicit opium, coca leaf and cannabis is still many times the amount currently consumed by drug abusers. Escalating demand offsets good efforts by many countries to reduce production through eradication."

However sincere, eradication drives are lagging far behind increases in crops.

Moreover, the drug trade has become an accepted fact of political life in some Latin American countries. Governments are overwhelmed by the sheer intractability of the problem, which is compounded by the growing significance of drug-related jobs and profits for several Latin American economies. Moreover, there are signs of a backlash in Latin America against drug-control policies that have become identified with external pressure, particularly from the United States.

Mexico, along with Colombia, is the focal point of U.S. attention to narcotics in Latin America. In the 1970s Mexico was a drug control success story. Energetic eradication efforts between the mid-1970s and 1983 sharply diminished Mexico's share of marijuana supplies to the U.S., from 70 percent to 10, and its share of U.S. heroin supplies tumbled from almost 90 percent to about one-third. Eradication is still a major priority for the Mexican government. More than half the Attorney General's $36 million budget in 1987 went to such operations, with the United States contributing some $15 million. About a fifth of Mexico's 125,000-man army was involved as well.

Despite these efforts, however, Mexico has again become the largest foreign source of heroin and marijuana for the U.S. market, and an estimated third of the cocaine reaching the United States transits that country. Part of the reason surely is Mexico's economic crisis, which encourages small farmers to return to lucrative drug crops just as it strains government resources for attacking the problem. U.S. officials also cite increasing corruption as a culprit. U.S. interdiction efforts in the southeastern United States, while inadequate to bite much into total drug supplies, did manage to push traffic westward, through Mexico, to the permeable border with the United States.

Mexico serves as a reminder that the situations of Latin American drug-producing countries vary considerably. The Andean producing countries, for example, have become genuinely alarmed by exploding narcotics abuse in their own countries; by contrast, drug abuse in Mexico—glue or concrete sniffing in urban slums more than cocaine or marijuana—is not yet a major social problem. While traffickers have corrupted Mexican institutions, nowhere do they pose a direct threat to government control, as they did in the 1970s in the "critical triangle" of Sinaloa, Durango and Chihuahua. By moving against drugs there, the central government also regained control where traffickers, perhaps mixed with anti-government guerrillas, had become a law unto themselves. Now, as one Mexican commentator put it: "Mexico has a drug problem. It is called the United States."

Colombia is a distant third to Peru and Bolivia in coca production, but it is the jumping-off point for perhaps three-quarters of all the cocaine smuggled into the United States. The administration of President Virgilio Barco has continued the war on drugs, but seems to be losing. The list of those assassinated by the traffickers is a who's who of Colombia's anti-drug campaigns: the former commander of the special anti-narcotics police, a supreme court justice, a premier journalist, and, most recently, the attorney general. One of the most infamous of the traffickers was arrested in early 1987 in the wake of an assassination attempt on a former Colombian justice minister, and immediately extradited to the United States. At the same time, though, other well-known traffickers remain free or have been released after brief confinement. Honest judges who sign extradition orders risk a death sentence from traffickers. In this atmosphere, Colombia's supreme court nullified the extradition treaty with the United States in February 1987.

In 1986, Colombia increased its eradication of marijuana by about half, to nearly 10,000 hectares. However, coca eradication slowed because the operations of anti-government guerrillas in coca producing regions made it too dangerous. For the same reason, drug seizures also dropped. The 1,500-man narcotics police suffered 58 casualties in 1986 alone.

For all the attention paid to links between traffickers and guerrillas in Latin America, the actual relationship is still unclear. It appears to vary from country to country, ranging from actual guerrilla involvement in trafficking, at one extreme, to violent conflict pitting traffickers and right-wing para-military groups against suspected guerrillas, at the other.

In the early 1980s, when cocaine became so plentiful that international prices dropped, Colombian traffickers began dumping coca leaf on the local market. It was fabricated into crude drugs called *bazucos*, highly addictive and all the more dangerous because of the additives—sulfuric acid, kerosene or gasoline—used in their production. By 1986 the Colombian health ministry estimated that as many as a half million of the country's 28 million people were regular bazuco smokers.

In response, Colombia has set up a program of extra-curricular activities for its teenagers, hoping to involve a sixth of its five million teenagers by the end of the year. Yet the program seems destined to reach middle-class youth who attend school and whose parents are as alarmed by spiralling drug use as their counterparts in the United States—not those poor children who remain on the streets surrounded by the drug culture.

Peru is the world's largest producer of coca leaf, with annual production in the range of 100 million metric tons. As in Colombia and Bolivia, drug-trafficking is mixed up in various ways with anti-government insurgencies while domestic drug abuse has become a major social problem. The Sendero Luminoso (Shining Path) insurgency has spread through much of the country, but it remains strongest in remote areas where the central government's authority is weak. Some of those areas, in particular north-eastern Peru and the upper Huallaga valley, are also drug-producing areas, and insurgents and traffickers often fall into tacit alliances against their common enemy—the government in Lima.

Since its inauguration in 1985, the administration of President Alán Garcia has conducted five major enforcement operations and, despite increasing violence, has persisted in eradication efforts. Yet confronted by a collapsing economy in addition to domestic violence, Peru, too, seems to be losing the drug war. The country is plagued by a major paradox of narcotics-control policies: the harsher the laws and penalties for drug trafficking, the greater the incentive for corruption.

Bolivia has made a remarkable rebound from its hyper-inflation; but its economy remains in desperate straits, and its drug-control successes have been meager. In 1986, Operation Blast Furnace, involving six U.S. Army helicopters with U.S. military and Drug Enforcement Administration (DEA) personnel, raided cocaine laboratories in the country's Beni region. The assault, however, came as no surprise to the traffickers, and so the amount of narcotics actually seized was modest. Still, the short-run disruption was significant: the facilities put out of business, albeit temporarily, had the capacity to process more than 20 percent of total U.S. consumption, and the local price of coca leaves dropped below production costs for a time. But the longer-term effect has been negligible. Coca prices began to rise in Bolivia as U.S. troops moved out, in the expectation that cocaine processing would begin again. And the flow of cocaine to the United States was undiminished.

If Bolivia has made no real progress in eradication recently, it is not hard to see why. The country's problem is less the mixing of traffickers and guerrillas—though there is some of that—than simple economics. The narcotics trade is so lucrative that traffickers can buy the protection they need. The coca crop is lucrative for peasants, too, compared to the alternatives. One estimate several years ago reckoned that producers in the Chapare region, where two-thirds of the nation's coca is grown, could earn almost twenty times more money cultivating coca than citrus, the next most profitable crop. And by working as *pisadores* (stompers of coca leaf), landless peasants can earn six to eight times what licit rural employment pays.

The Latin American narcotics network keeps spreading. Citizens of the Dominican Republic now hold a share of trafficking to the United States, once monopolized by Colombians and Cuban-Americans. Countries as far apart as the Bahamas and Argentina have become significant sites for refining and trans-shipment. Panama has become a focal point for laundering drug profits, as underscored by the recent U.S. indictment of the country's *de facto* ruler, General Manuel Antonio Noriega.

Paraguay and Brazil have recently become involved in both production and trafficking. The former, the base of the French Connection in the 1970s, now exports several thousand tons of marijuana, virtually all of it to South America and most of it to Brazil. One side effect of Operation Blast Furnace in Bolivia may have been to stimulate new cocaine processing facilities in the adjacent Chaco region of Paraguay. Even Brazil, which neither depends much on drug income nor lacks the means to control its territory, halted coca eradication when heavily-armed Colombian guerrillas moved into the target areas for rest and resupply.

Where We Stand in the Hemisphere

Narcotics has emerged as a major issue in hemispheric relations. For some drug-producing countries, it has become the single most important issue affecting their relations with the United States. The Anti-Drug Abuse Act of 1986 required the U.S. President to pressure Latin American drug-producing countries in a number of ways: compelling him to certify Bolivia's anti-drug efforts before resuming aid to that country; withholding $1 million in drug aid to Mexico until he reported on Mexican progress in bringing the killers of Drug Enforcement Agency (DEA) official Enrique Camarena to justice; and suggesting that the President should consider additional sanctions against Mexico—a travel advisory and other cuts in aid, multilateral bank loans and trade benefits.

The Act also required U.S. representatives in multilateral development banks to vote against loans to any country whose anti-drug programs the President did not certify. Separately, the law denied sugar quotas and imposed up to 50 percent tariffs on the exports of countries whose programs the President did not determine to be adequate. Those determinations, moreover, could be overridden by joint Congressional resolutions.

In 1987, the President denied certification only to Iran, Afghanistan and Syria—none of which received U.S. assistance in any case. Members of Congress failed to override the President's certification of Mexico, Panama and the Bahamas, and the Senate instead voted to compel the President to re-examine the certification. But the episode demonstrated how much inter-American relations could be affected by passions over the drug issue.

On the positive side, the hemispheric community took a modest step in 1987 by creating the Inter-American Drug Abuse Control Commission (CICAD). CICAD is untested, and its budget is small, but it signals recognition that the drug problem must be addressed in its hemispheric dimensions. CICAD envisions a training center and, more promising, an Inter-American Documentation Center to serve as a resource for member countries. If this sharing of information among countries of the Hemisphere could lay the basis for evaluation of what works and what does not, it could be particularly valuable.

Coping with Narcotics

Progress in confronting the drug problem will be slow; simply containing its growth would constitute success beyond current expectations. However, recent experience teaches one clear lesson: supply-side policies by themselves do not work. Primary attention must shift to demand. As long as the profit margin for cocaine is 12,000 percent from production cost to street value, the lure of trafficking will be irresistible, and "narco-dollars" will buy all the protection drug lords need. Yet from 1981 to 1987, while federal aid for drug enforcement in the United States more than doubled, support for prevention, education and treatment remained static at about $400 million.

Experience has shown time and again that short-term disruptions of drug supplies have little or no long-term effect on drug availability in the United States. Eradication programs temporarily succeeded in Mexico and Bolivia—and previously in Turkey—but failed ultimately to reduce the flood of illegal drugs to the United States. It is all too easy for drug traffickers to shift their sources of supply from country to country and, if necessary, from continent to continent, one step ahead of U.S.-assisted drug enforcement programs.

If any inroads are to be made, the Hemisphere's approach to the narcotics issue should be based on three guidelines:

- The single most important priority is for the United States to focus on containing its own demand for narcotics. More money must be allocated to programs for prevention and rehabilitation, and more research must be done to determine what specific measures are most effective in reducing demand.

- U.S. pressure on Latin American governments has probably led to more vigorous efforts to eradicate and seize crops, but it has not put any real dent in the supply of drugs in the Hemisphere or lessened the crime and corruption associated with drugs. *The United States should help countries to design and implement their own drug-control policies, rather than apply pressure and threaten sanctions if countries do not adopt U.S. prescriptions.*

- Inter-American cooperation to deal with drugs must be based on honest assessments of the problem by all countries of the Hemisphere.

Containing U.S. Demand

If the war on drugs is ever to be won, the United States has no alternative but to curb its demand for illegal drugs. If demand remains high, even "sealing" U.S. borders, were that possible, would only shift supply to domestically-grown substances or to so-called "designer drugs" made from chemicals. The campaign against imports already has had unintended, and sometimes perverse, results: because efforts to interdict imported drugs have been more successful against marijuana than against the less bulky and more lucrative cocaine, many traffickers have switched to cocaine. As a result, up to half the marijuana used in the United States may now be homegrown.

Anti-smoking and anti-marijuana campaigns provide some suggestions and some hope for reducing demand, but the exact ingredients for success are still a mystery. Daily cigarette smoking among teenagers, for example, dropped by a third between 1977 and 1981. Yet, despite intensive anti-smoking campaigns, there has been almost no decline since then. So, too, marijuana use among U.S. teenagers fell sharply between the mid-1970s and the mid-1980s, but no one knows how much of that apparent reduction reflected a switch to cocaine and alcohol.

The U.S. government should assign high and sustained priority to drug education and rehabilitation programs. But more research is needed to make those programs more effective. There are still major uncertainties about what works and why. It is imperative to improve understanding of how the drug problem relates to other social problems, especially among adolescents, and what approaches can best attack these interrelated problems.

It may also be useful to begin distinguishing among different drugs. Social attitudes toward marijuana vary greatly from those toward heroin, for example. And the consequences for users and for society as a whole are vastly different. Moreover, there is a difference between the damage caused by the use of drugs and the harm that results from their illegality. It is premature to contemplate legalizing any dangerous drug—but it might be sensible to examine carefully all of the likely consequences, positive and negative, of selective legislation.

Reducing Counterproductive Pressure
on Foreign Suppliers

Most independent analysts are skeptical about the utility of supply reduction, but that view has not had much influence on U.S. policy debates. Understanding of the issue—in the U.S. Congress, for instance—remains scanty. <u>The New York Times</u> editorial cited earlier sounded a clarion call for "stopping foreign drugs flowing into our country...at the source, not at our border or in the streets of American cities." Even inside the U.S. executive branch, overseas drug eradication receives most attention, almost independent of its effect.

Eradicating Latin American drug crops, however, has had virtually no impact on drug supplies in the United States. World drug production is too high to expect eradication efforts to affect U.S. consumption. Current U.S. pressures to eliminate crops may risk discrediting U.S. anti-drug efforts generally. They will certainly not solve the drug problems of either the United States or Latin America. Latin American countries should instead be encouraged and assisted to develop sensible multi-faceted strategies to deal with *their* drug situation.

Latin American drug-producing countries face a range of different problems and confront different economic and political constraints in their efforts to deal with drugs. Eradication and seizure could be a useful part of a more general strategy for some of those countries. These actions might well help them cope with their domestic drug problems; since they are at the low-price end of the market, local production destroyed is not likely to be replaced by imports from abroad. Operation Blast Furnace did raise drug prices in Bolivia, albeit temporarily, while it had no effect on those in the United States.

Some rethinking of existing strategies—with their heavy emphasis on eradication and thus on visible cooperation with U.S. authorities—is underway in many countries of the region. Mexican students of the problem, for instance, have suggested retargeting their national effort away from eradicating marijuana and toward disrupting trafficking networks, especially for heroin. The central point is that decisions to cooperate with the United States should be national choices, not concessions to external political pressures. The United States needs to remember that narcotics, although an urgent concern, is not the only issue on the Hemisphere's agenda. Frictions over drugs should not hamper cooperation on other critical problems.

Facing the Problem Honestly

If a cooperative, hemispheric approach to narcotics is to take hold, all countries, North and South, must face the issue honestly. The drug problem is deadly serious and will not be solved quickly or easily. The fact is that there are currently no good solutions, and conventional approaches such as eradication have not been effective. No nation by itself can solve the narcotics problem, and all nations must avoid inflated rhetoric and finger-pointing. Only if each country of the Hemisphere concentrates on doing what it can internally to confront this affliction can Latin America and the United States turn what is now a shared tragedy into an opportunity for cooperation.

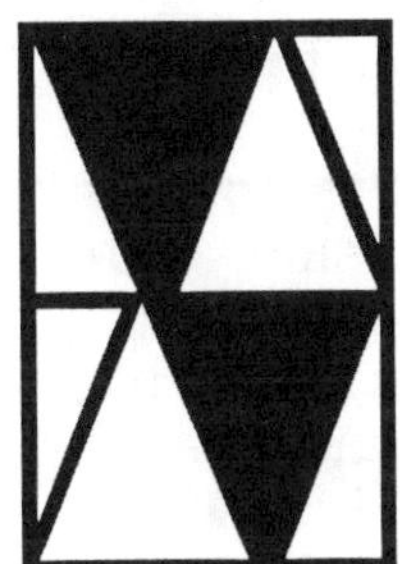

Chapter IV

Migration: Problem or Solution?

The Americas are, and always have been, a region of people on the move. Our Hemisphere has been built by migration, by the steady flow of people to new colonies and new countries, and by an equally steady flow from coastal settlements to interior frontiers and then from farmlands to the cities. The ancestors of many millions of our Hemisphere's citizens came to these shores against their will, brought here as slaves. But most of the people of the Americas descend from migrants who came to the New World by choice, in search of economic opportunity, freedom, security, or simply to begin a new life. The right to migrate has long been valued in the Western Hemisphere.

For three hundred years, the international migration affecting the Americas was mostly from the Old World to the New. This flow continues. A day spent in Los Angeles, Toronto or Sao Paulo reminds one that this Hemisphere is still a magnet for people from all around the world. In recent years, however, international migration in the Western Hemisphere has been dominated by people moving within the region—among the countries of Latin America and the Caribbean, and from these countries to the United States and Canada.

As the countries of origin have changed, so have the causes of migration, and, even more so, attitudes toward migrants. For most of the past century, migration had been viewed, by and large, as a solution more than a problem. Economic downturns have, from time to time, spawned exclusionary sentiments, which too often were expressed in racist terms. But for the most part, immigration was considered a favorable reflection on the New World's opportunities and freedoms.

In recent years, however, prevailing attitudes toward migration have changed. Demographic explosion, economic recession, social upheaval, and political turmoil have transformed the context. Since 1950, Latin America's population has more than doubled; this surge has created an enormous demand for jobs in the 1980s, just when economic growth in the region has slowed. Meanwhile, advances in transportation and communications have made migration easier. And political violence has uprooted hundreds of thousands of Central Americans, adding a major new pressure for migration.

As the flow of migrants has expanded, resistance to immigration has begun to build in the receiving countries. Greater pressures to move, combined with mounting resentment toward the resulting flows, are heightening hemispheric tensions. Uncontrolled and undesired migration could ignite worse conflicts, damaging to both sending and receiving countries—and to the migrants themselves. Hemispheric cooperation is needed to reduce these tensions and to assure that migration remains a valued aspect of life in the Americas.

Governments in the Hemisphere must recognize that large-scale cross-border migration flows are likely to persist for many years. This is not cause for alarm. Such flows, particularly if they are regulated and predictable, can benefit the Americas, bringing labor markets into better balance, easing a variety of social and economic strains, and improving the lives of countless individuals.

In seeking positive approaches to migration, it is crucial to understand the complex motives that cause people to migrate: some are seeking to rejoin their families; others want to improve their economic situation; and still others are fleeing violence and repression. Often a combination of circumstances propels people to move.

Economic Migration

Most migration in the Hemisphere is motivated by economic considerations. People leave areas of underemployment and low wages for places where they can find work that is better paid. Reinforcing this labor migration have been loose border controls and migratory traditions that have created strong social and economic ties between particular geographic regions in sending countries and specific labor markets in receiving countries.

Currently the Hemisphere's largest labor migration is from Mexico to the United States. Its antecedents include the *bracero* program, a legal temporary-worker arrangement that brought some five million Mexican farm workers to the United States between 1942 and 1964. This program created a strong interdependence between agriculture in the southwestern United States and rural peasant communities in several Mexican states.

Today, the flow from Mexico is largely illegal. Of an estimated four to six million undocumented aliens in the United States, more than half are labor migrants from Mexico.

Rural workers seeking temporary, often seasonal, jobs still account for much of the Mexican labor migration. But the stream has broadened to include urban migrants who are better educated and have greater occupational skills. Unlike most migrant farm workers, they come to the United States with their families and settle in major American cities, finding jobs that are mostly shunned by American workers.

Contrary to popular belief, undocumented workers in the United States today are usually paid the legal minimum wage or better, although still less than the prevailing wage rate. U.S. wages are relatively so large—more than 15 times those in Mexico in some occupations—that the lure of the U.S. job market is overpowering. Nonetheless, living outside the law makes migrants vulnerable to abuse and exploitation. Many illegal residents live in poverty, with scant access to even minimal social services.

Labor migration has produced important changes in both the United States and Mexico. Northward migration is now a Mexican institution. Whole communities depend on remittances to supplement family incomes. The debt-ridden Mexican economy depends heavily on them as well. An estimated $1 to $1.5 billion of annual remittances are the country's fourth largest source of foreign exchange, after oil, manufacturing exports, and tourism.

The Mexican labor force will swell by nearly one million persons each year until the end of the century, when the effect of declining birth rates on employment should be felt. If Mexico could achieve an annual economic growth rate of five percent, considerably above the one percent it has averaged in the 1980s, this would still generate only 800,000 new jobs a year. Thus, even with a much healthier economy, Mexico would have a massive employment problem, and migration would remain the only alternative to joblessness or underemployment for many thousands of Mexicans.

Until recently, it has been relatively easy to migrate from Mexico to the United States. It is still early to be sure how that migration will be affected by the new limits that the United States imposed when the Immigration Reform and Control Act of 1986 (IRCA)* was adopted. These controls are unlikely to stop migration, but they may somewhat reduce the flow, at least for a time. Mexico's employment problems would then loom larger, and the country's work force may become more restive. Bilateral relations would surely be affected.

Labor migration from the Caribbean islands presents a different picture. These islands have been more deeply and continuously affected by international migration than any region in the Hemisphere. Migration is an integral part of Caribbean economies. Several smaller islands have become remittance societies, with money from abroad providing the largest single source of income.

Historically, Caribbean countries have been nations of both immigration and emigration, but since the 1940s the movement has been largely outward. Some 10 percent of those born in the region now live abroad, mainly in the United States and Canada. But the flow of Caribbean

---

* The Immigration Reform and Control Act of 1986 (IRCA), the most sweeping reform of U.S. immigration policy in the last 35 years, became law in November 1986. Its key provisions establish, for the first time, legal penalties for employers who knowingly hire undocumented workers and offer opportunities for certain groups of undocumented migrants to acquire legal status.

migrants has also reached Mexico, Colombia, and Venezuela. And large numbers of Haitians, fleeing abject poverty and political repression in their homeland, have settled next door in the Dominican Republic.

Labor migration is also extensive in South America. Venezuela and Argentina receive many migrants from neighboring countries. At times, Venezuela has had as many as two to four million illegal residents out of a total population of less than 20 million. Most of these have been Colombians, but they have included Ecuadorans, Peruvians, and Dominicans as well. In Argentina, with 31 million people, the illegal immigrant population has been estimated to be 1.5 to three million persons, principally Bolivians, Chileans, Paraguayans, and Uruguayans.

Like the United States, Venezuela and Argentina officially oppose uncontrolled migration. Yet just as in North America, certain regions within these countries lack unskilled and semi-skilled labor, especially for temporary or seasonal jobs. The Argentine government has responded by creating programs to help industries hire foreign temporary workers when the demand has been greatest. Venezuela has from time to time allowed large increases in the undocumented population because of labor needs. Regulation and enforcement, in other words, are influenced by economic considerations.

For all the recent emphasis on problems caused by illegal foreign populations, labor migration often facilitates economic and social adjustments in sending and receiving countries alike. Emigration is a way that societies contend with widespread poverty and explosive labor force growth. Yet emigration can carry a steep price tag; sending countries lose ambitious people and talented citizens, mainly young people just entering their most productive years. These costs have been especially heavy for several Caribbean states.

Receiving countries benefit when migrants fill vacant jobs and bolster productivity in certain geographic areas and economic sectors. Further, migrants as a whole probably pay more in taxes than they receive in services. In areas where migrants concentrate, however, exceptional burdens can fall on hard-pressed local governments. Hospitals and schools, in particular, often become overcrowded. Illegal migrants mostly take jobs that would, in their absence, remain unfilled or disappear, but in some cases they do displace native workers.

The fundamental objection to undocumented migration is political, not economic. The very fact of illegality is what most troubles governments and local populations. When a country cannot control who enters and who remains in its territory, the government and its citizens feel vulnerable, and at times, threatened and overwhelmed. They sometimes resent illegal entrants as intruders, particularly those that are ethnically, culturally and linguistically different. Resentment tends to be greatest in areas where illegal migrants concentrate and among low-income groups who see migrants competing for jobs and depressing wages. Even in nations that are proud of a diverse ethnic and cultural heritage, new and uninvited groups may provoke strong nationalistic sentiments.

Countries have tried to control illegal migration in a variety of ways, including border enforcement, employment regulations, and amnesty programs. Argentina, Canada, Venezuela, and the United States have all experimented with combinations of these measures. The crucial fact, however, is that immigration policies are almost wholly based on the domestic considerations of receiving states, even though countries of origin also have major interests at stake.

Latin American reactions to the 1986 U.S. law suggest that sending states want a voice on U.S. immigration policies and those of other receiving countries. The Dominican Republic dispatched a commission to Washington to request an "elastic" application of the new U.S. law. Two Central American presidents appealed to the United States not to deport migrants from the region. These actions may signal an important shift in the behavior of sending countries. If the trend were to continue, they might one day openly seek from receiving countries easier entry for their nationals, greater protection of migrants' rights, and other immigration policy changes.

Labor migration is now woven tightly into the economic fabric of much of the Hemisphere. Its causes are long-term

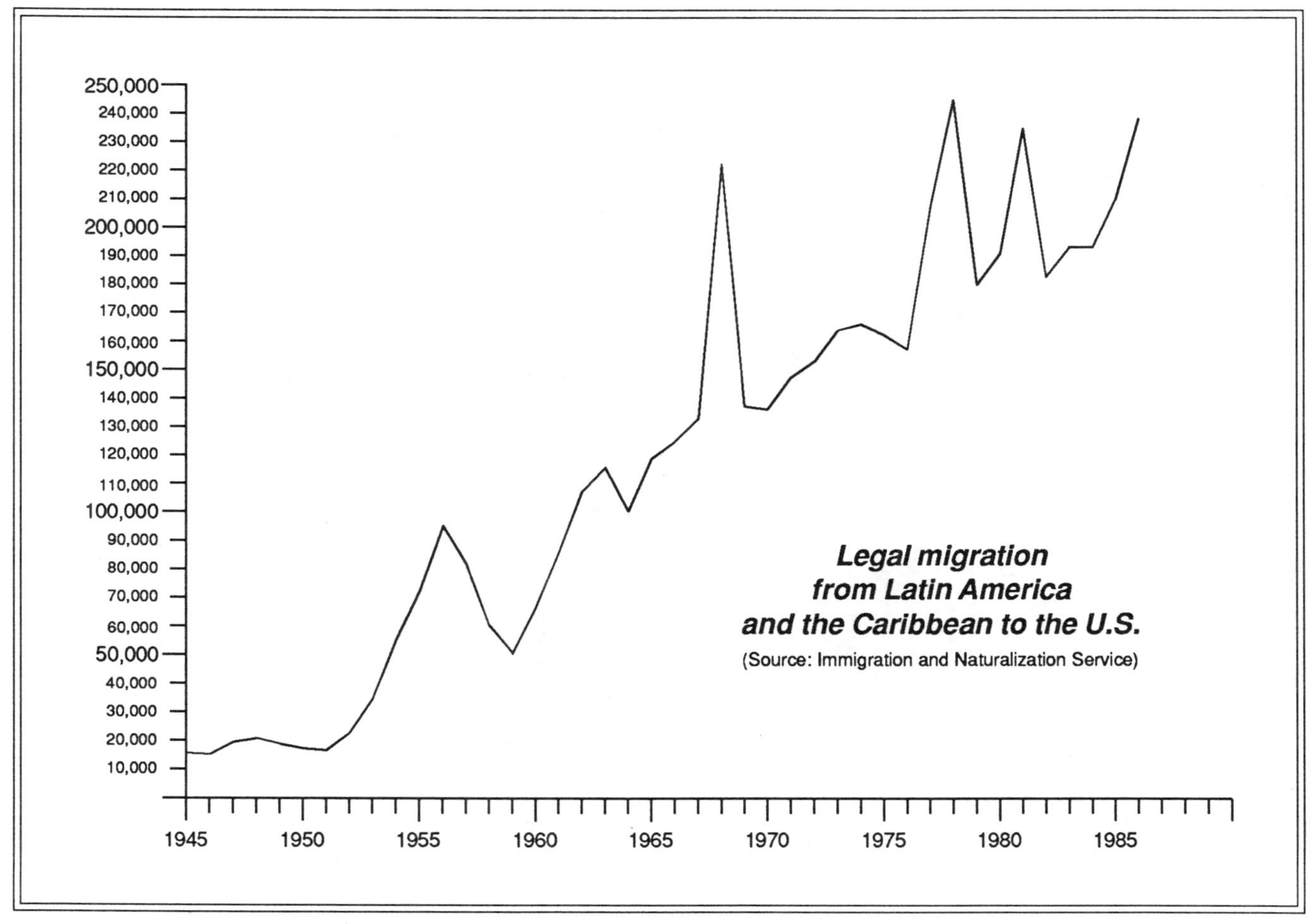

250,000
240,000
230,000
220,000
210,000
200,000
190,000
180,000
170,000
160,000
150,000
140,000
130,000
120,000
110,000
100,000
90,000
80,000
70,000
60,000
50,000
40,000
30,000
20,000
10,000
1945
1950
1955
1960
1965
1970
1975
1980
1985
Legal migration
from Latin America
and the Caribbean to the U.S.
(Source: Immigration and Naturalization Service)

and structural, and they will persist and perhaps intensify. Once established, migration streams perpetuate themselves. Large-scale labor migration has become an inescapable reality of inter-American affairs.

Politically Motivated Migration

Political violence and oppression have also been a major cause of migration in the Hemisphere. Tens of thousands of people, for example, fled the harsh dictatorships of South America's Southern Cone countries in the 1960 and the 1970s. More than one million Cubans have left their island since Fidel Castro took power in 1959. Other large flows of migrants, particularly from Haiti and Central America, have been motivated by a combination of political and economic factors.

Migration both among Central American countries and from the region is not new. For centuries, peasants from crowded El Salvador have moved across porous borders to seek land in less populated Guatemala and Honduras. The Indians of the Misquito coast on Central America's eastern shores have traditionally moved freely between Honduras and Nicaragua. Guatemalans have long migrated into southern Mexico as seasonal farm laborers. Modest numbers of Central Americans made their way to the United States beginning in the early 1970s. But Costa Rica, Honduras and Nicaragua had not experienced large scale emigration until recently.

Today's massive movements from and within Central America are less than ten years old. The economic distress, political repression and civil violence that permeate the region are mutually reinforcing motivations for flight. Since 1980, nearly one million Central Americans have been displaced within their own countries and another one to 1.7 million have fled to other countries in the region and outside. More than 60 percent of the uprooted are Salvadorans, representing about one-quarter of that country's population, and most of the rest are Nicaraguans.

The refugees' primary destinations within the region are Honduras and Costa Rica, both nations which extend first asylum status, i.e., temporary safety, to the displaced.

Honduras hosts about 70,000 persons from Nicaragua, El Salvador and Guatemala; Costa Rica about 100,000, mostly Nicaraguans. But these are less than 15 percent of Central America's refugees. The rest have fled mainly to Mexico, Canada, and the United States. No precise accounting is available, but estimates suggest that at least 150,000 and perhaps as many as 400,000 Salvadorans and Guatemalans are in Mexico, and between 700,000 and 1.2 million Salvadorans, Guatemalans, Hondurans and Nicaraguans live in the United States and Canada.

International law currently assigns refugee status to persons with a "well-founded fear of persecution" based on race, religion, nationality, political opinion, or membership in a social group. Some uprooted Central Americans are refugees in this sense. But the great majority have no recourse to formal refugee status under international norms. They have emigrated due to political events in which they were only marginally involved, if at all. The United States and most other governments withhold refugee status and its protections from migrants escaping political turmoil, civil strife, natural disaster, and the economic decline that usually accompanies such profound disruptions of normal life.

Parts of Central America have become dangerous and inhospitable, if not virtually uninhabitable, especially for the poor. The hundreds of thousands of people who have fled those areas deserve humane and intelligent treatment. Most of them are now living in conditions of extreme poverty and deprivation. Jobs and social services are scarce in their countries of refuge, and they are fearful of returning home to even worse conditions.

So far the response to Central America's displaced has been piecemeal and inadequate. Each Central American country has taken steps to accommodate refugees without actually granting them legal status. The United Nations High Commission for Refugees (UNHCR) administers camps and provides protection in the region for a small minority of the displaced. Canada has offered safe haven, but has recently placed greater restrictions on entry. Except for Nicaraguans, the United States has been very restrictive in its asylum policy. Washington formally denies the political dimension of Central American migration, and reserves the right to expel undocumented migrants from the region—although U.S. authorities have forced only a small fraction to return.

The Central American countries and Mexico have sought regional solutions to the refugee problem. In November 1984, the states of Central America and the members of the Contadora Group (Mexico, Panama, Colombia, and Venezuela) agreed to the Cartagena Declaration on Refugees, which establishes a framework for more humane treatment of Central America's displaced. The Declaration's key provision proposes "enlarging the concept of a refugee" to include those fleeing because their "lives, safety or freedom have been threatened by generalized violence, foreign aggression, internal conflicts, massive violation of human rights or other circumstances." Although the UNHCR has not adopted the Declaration, it was endorsed by the five Central American presidents in the Guatemala peace plan.

As we have emphasized in Chapter One, so long as Central America remains at war, there can be no solution to the region's refugee problems. But peace will not necessarily resolve the problems either. If the region's conflicts were settled, many refugees would seek to return home; but they would face shortages of jobs, land, housing, and public services. After seven years of economic stagnation, no Central American country can easily accommodate returning citizens. The region's per capita output has plunged by nearly 25 percent since 1981; unemployment and underemployment are widespread; and poverty is deeper than ever. Refugee problems compound—and are compounded by—Central America's political turmoil and its economic and social distress.

Emigration from Haiti resembles the recent experience of Central America. Many thousands of rural laborers from Haiti's impoverished countryside have long moved in search of work—mainly to the sugar plantations of the neighboring Dominican Republic, but elsewhere in the Caribbean as well. Since 1958, when François Duvalier ("Papa Doc") came to power, official repression, terror and corruption joined grinding poverty to motivate Haitian migration—and an increasing share of this migration began to flow to the United States.

For many years, the pattern was for Haitians to travel to the United States on visitors' visas and then remain in the country. In 1972, migrants from Haiti began arriving in South Florida in boats. Their numbers increased markedly after 1977, reaching some 25,000 in 1980. Although clearly fleeing political oppression as well as economic hardship, the boat people—poor, unskilled, and black—were not welcomed. After several years of legal and political controversy over how to deal with the situation, the United States in 1981, under an agreement signed with Haiti, began intercepting Haitian vessels before they reached U.S. territorial waters and forcing their return to Haiti. Boat arrivals have dropped dramatically since interdiction began.

Cuba presents a special case. Migration from that country since the revolution of 1959 has mostly been driven by politics, although family reunification has also played a role. The movement from Cuba has been a stop-and-go affair, depending on Cuban government decisions to prohibit, allow, or even promote emigration and on U.S. willingness to authorize refugee admissions. The flow was suspended for most of this decade following the Mariel episode of 1980, when Cuba encouraged the exodus of nearly 125,000 people to the United States, including perhaps several thousand criminals and mentally ill persons. The U.S. government declared these persons ineligible for entry, has kept many of them in detention, and halted further migration until Cuba accepted their return.

In late 1987, the United States and Cuba finally agreed to regularize migration. The Cuban government offered to repatriate nearly 3,000 of the detained Marielitos, and the United States began admitting former political prisoners and up to 20,000 other Cubans eligible for entry under the standard immigration quota that applies to all countries.

A Policy Framework and Recommendations

International migration throughout the Hemisphere will be significant into the foreseeable future. The nations of the Hemisphere must find ways to cope with this flow of people. *We must learn to manage the tension and instability, both domestic and international, caused by migration—and must undertake efforts to improve the conditions of migrants and refugees throughout the Americas.*

Migration Policy-making: Migration policy will mainly be driven by domestic considerations. Control over the entry of non-citizens is everywhere considered a fundamental element of national sovereignty. Nevertheless, migration problems require greater cooperation among affected nations in the Hemisphere.

- Migration policy-making should involve broader consultation among sending and receiving countries. Changes in law and policy should be preceded by detailed exchanges of information and careful examination of expected ramifications. The United States and the major countries of origin should establish formal mechanisms to conduct such exchanges on a regular basis.

    The United States should initiate consultations with sending nations to review policy and administrative issues posed by the new U.S. immigration law. It would be useful to begin with a broad assessment of the law's impact both on the United States and on the countries of origin. Other items for discussion might include: the evidence required to prove eligibility for amnesty, rules governing family members of persons qualified for amnesty, the treatment of migrants ineligible for legal status, enforcement and deportation practices, border enforcement techniques, and the application and likely effects of employer sanctions.

    U.S. opinion continues to be divided over the new law. Many employers seem to be complying with the hiring restrictions on undocumented persons, but some evasion is also taking place. In Latin America and the Caribbean, attitudes toward the law and its restrictions are generally unfavorable. Mexican officials have criticized its passage as an unfriendly act against Mexico because it is intended to reduce migrant flows. These officials also predict that the law will not, in fact, do much to stem illegal entry because economic incentives for migration remain so strong.

Such clashing perceptions underscore the need for sustained attention from authorities in both the United States and sending countries. Diplomacy will not solve all problems, but the sharing of information and opinions should permit greater accommodation and help avoid misunderstandings.

• Migration policy should be free from the xenophobia that too often permeates popular feelings on the issue. Attitudes in receiving countries will always be affected by nationalist sentiments and resentment of outsiders, but political leaders and government officials must avoid policies and rhetoric that pander to such attitudes.

• Migration policies must take account of economic needs in both receiving and sending countries. For example, the special agricultural worker (SAW) provision* of the new U.S. immigration law, with all its imperfections, at least recognizes that a significant sector of the U.S. economy depends on Mexican labor. Intended mainly to ensure a steady labor supply to the Southwestern United States, the SAW provision is also consistent with Mexico's interests, and shows that national policies can be sensitive to particular migration flows. There should be more such pragmatically determined migration programs in the Hemisphere, negotiated, whenever possible, within a bilateral framework.

• Governments must give greater protection to the human rights and basic needs of undocumented migrants throughout the Hemisphere. Too often illegal migrants and their families live in appalling conditions. They are overcharged for cramped, unsanitary housing, exploited at work, and excluded from social assis-

---

* The SAW provision of the Immigration Reform and Control Act of 1986 allows some undocumented agricultural workers to obtain legal status and permits the entry of new workers if shortages appear.

tance programs. Receiving countries should take greater responsibility for protecting migrants against such abuses, and countries of origin should assist their nationals in foreign states.

Migrants do have certain internationally recognized human rights that must be respected. They cannot, for instance, lawfully be deprived of wages they have earned. If arrested, they must be advised of their circumstances in a language they understand. Yet difficult questions remain about the extent of migrants' rights, and these are being debated and litigated in many countries of the Hemisphere. Should undocumented aliens, for example, have a right to education and health care services?

Many of the questions have been addressed in detail by European governments in their long effort to establish free movement and economic cooperation. Two International Labor Organization conventions, in 1952 and 1978, codified an important body of principles and practices for coping with large-scale migration. Western Hemisphere governments and regional organizations, such as the Organization of American States (OAS) and the Inter-American Commission for Human Rights, should follow the European example. Codification of migrant rights is an important step toward framing bilateral or multilateral agreements that can effectively protect those rights.

Sending countries could help by instructing their diplomats to serve as advocates for migrant rights. Mexico has begun to adopt this approach. In concert with the consulates of El Salvador, Colombia, Honduras and Guatemala, Mexican diplomats last year joined in a Houston lawsuit to "safeguard the rights and privileges" of illegal migrants in the United States. The verdict now prevents employers from summarily firing aliens who are eligible for amnesty under the new immigration law. Also in Houston, Mexico is participating in a project to prepare a "black list" of unscrupulous immigration consultants and attorneys known to provide inaccurate information or charge excessive fees.

- Better monitoring is needed to determine the effects of national policies and other events on migration flows and the situation of migrants. At the urging of Latin American labor ministers, the OAS created a migration program six years ago which now provides country-by-country analyses of migration movements and relevant legal issues. It also offers assistance and training to government officials in techniques of measuring migration. The OAS program should be expanded to include regular reporting on a wider range of migration matters and on significant research results.

  Improved research on the causes and consequences of migration would help to improve future policy. How do the political and economic impulses to migrate interact? What is the amount and significance of remittances for different countries? What factors prompt or discourage return mi-gration and how serious are adjustment problems? What are the working and living conditions of migrants in different receiving countries?

Refugees and Displaced Persons: The massive refugee-like movements within and from Central America merit urgent attention. The best framework for addressing the problems is the Cartagena Declaration on Refugees, which urges a broad definition of refugees that encompasses persons fleeing generalized violence and massive human rights violations.

- The Declaration should formally be ratified, at least by the Latin American nations that have endorsed it, and implementation procedures should be spelled out. Even if Canada and the United States are not willing to accept the broadened definition of refugees, they should not oppose adoption of the Declaration by the Latin American countries or the involvement of the United Nations High Commission for Refugees (UNHCR) in its implementation.

- The nations of Latin America have responded commendably to refugee movements, but their efforts have been limited to providing temporary safe haven. Even the Cartagena Declaration does not address the issue of permanent resettlement. In the Central American peace plan as well, the stated policy objective is repatriation. But many displaced persons will not or cannot return to their country of origin. Central American nations should recognize that many refugees will choose to resettle in their current location, and that policies on legal status and economic aid will have to be established for them. International support will be needed to assist both resettlement and repatriation efforts in Central America.

● Most displaced Central Americans reside in Mexico and the United States, both of which have refused to grant them asylum. Claims for political asylum should now be re-examined and decided using a more generous standard, as the United States has done for Nicaraguan applicants. Both Mexico and the United States should suspend routine deportations to the region, and allow for the permanent resettlement of Central Americans who have lived in the two countries for three years or more. Moreover, the United States, Mexico, and Canada should accept applications for refugee status from persons now in UNHCR camps in Central America.

Next Steps for U.S. Immigration Policy: Because the United States is the main destination of international migrants in the Hemisphere, U.S. policies are particularly significant. The United States should now take several important complementary steps to improve its new immigration law.

● *Extending Amnesty.* The amnesty provisions of IRCA were an important advance in U.S. immigration policy. They will provide legal status to as many as 1.5 million currently undocumented persons and begin a process to grant them permanent residency and eventually full citizenship in the United States. These provisions must be generously implemented so their benefits are available to all those who are eligible. We welcome the U.S. government's recent decision to extend the deadline for completed applications for two additional months, and would encourage further extension, as may be necessary, to increase participation. But even so, more than one-half of all illegal residents will not qualify because they arrived after the present 1982 cut-off date. Consideration should now be given to broadening the amnesty provisions, for example, by fixing a cut-off date much closer to the present and by relaxing some of the more restrictive regulations governing eligibility. This would enable a larger share of undocumented aliens to legalize their situations.

- *Revision of the rules governing family reunification.* Current law permits certain relatives of U.S. residents to immigrate to the United States. With perhaps one and a half million people about to gain legal residency through the amnesty provisions of IRCA, the demand for immigration of relatives could be overwhelming. The waiting periods for visas, already up to ten years for applicants from some countries, may become prohibitive. The period for family reunification— for those now waiting and for new applicants— should be reduced to a maximum of three to five years so that this barrier to legal migration does not generate a massive new illegal flow.

- *Authorization of some economic immigration.* U.S. immigration law has three objectives: to reunify families, offer safety to refugees, and supply needed workers. But in practice, the law permits only family reunification and refugee admission because applicants in these categories alone fill the legal quotas. Thus economic migration, except for farm workers under the SAW provision and highly-skilled labor, has been almost exclusively illegal. The U.S. Congress is presently reviewing several proposals to open legal avenues for economically-motivated migration. Where such migration can benefit both the United States and the sending countries, it should be facilitated.

71

- *A special approach for Mexico.* The United States should consider special policies toward Mexico, which is the source of more than half of all illegal immigration to the United States. Today, every country has the same numerical quota of 20,000 immigrants per year—placing large, neighboring Mexico, on the same footing, for example, as tiny, remote Botswana. Such non-discriminatory treatment may be attractive in theory, but it ignores reality. The United States and Mexico should jointly consider new arrangements, including the possibility of increased immigration quotas, that reflect and build on the extensive economic inter-dependence that binds them. Other pairs of countries in analogous situations, such as Haiti and the Dominican Republic, Bolivia and Argentina, and Colombia and Venezuela, should also consider special bilateral arrangements.

- *Information-sharing and research.* IRCA established a Commission for the Study of International Migration and Cooperative Economic Development to examine the conditions in countries of origin that spur unauthorized migration, to develop proposals for recip-rocal trade and investment programs to help to allevi-ate such conditions, and to explore the establishment of a comprehensive information exchange program between the United States and major sending coun-tries. This effort deserves close attention by the next U.S. Administration, to which its recommendations will be delivered.

Sending Nations: It is encouraging that some sending countries have begun to shed their traditional passivity toward migration and to formulate their own policies. Such efforts could help influence the policy decisions of the United States and other receiving states, which have to date addressed migration unilaterally as a domestic issue.

Besides seeking to shape the decisions of receiving nations, countries of origin must also look to their own policies. Development plans too often count on substantial emigration to alleviate labor surpluses. Greater attention to domestic employment generation and special rural development programs is particularly warranted. Counting on the United States and other receiving countries as an outlet for jobless workers is not a responsible approach. It leaves the sending countries' economic prospects, and even their political stability, hostage to the changing economic and political circumstances of receiving nations.

Politically-motivated migration can usually be traced to the actions of non-democratic and abusive governments. Governments that restrict political freedoms and violate the human rights of their citizens flout the values of the entire inter-American community. We strongly encourage support for the work of both official and private organizations that promote respect for human rights without partisan or ideological favor.

Finally, sending nations should develop policies for assisting the repatriation of their nationals seeking to return home. No one should be denied that right or hampered in their efforts to reside in their country of citizenship. Cooperation between sending and receiving countries can be helpful in addressing the problems associated with return migration.

Political and Social Integration: Large-scale immigration has a significant impact on every part of a country's life. The issues involved in temporary or seasonal migration are mainly economic: eligibility for employment, wages and work conditions, and the sending of remittances. Wider and more difficult issues must be faced when migration streams mature and large numbers of migrants decide to settle permanently in their new locations. Questions arise concerning access to social services, education for children, and eligibility for entitlement programs. Still more complex are issues regarding the social and political integration of migrants, for instance, their right to reunite their families, to join labor unions, and to participate in the politics of their new country.

Ultimately, every nation must decide for itself what it means for an individual or family to "belong" to its society, and how to deal with the situation of people who are physically present but barred from full social and political participation. The challenge is especially vexing for the pluralistic societies of the Western Hemisphere that are religiously, ethnically and racially diverse. These nations work best when all groups share a commitment to basic national ideals and actively participate in civic and political life. If the nations of the Hemisphere do not squarely confront this challenge, the flows of migrants may become a source of increasing tension and conflict between and within countries, and the migrants themselves will be cheated.

For the United States and Canada, difficult philosophic and political choices have already begun to emerge from large, uncontrolled migration flows. Institutions of representative government and the rule of law can have little meaning for illegal migrants who have virtually no recourse to those institutions or that law. The democratic values that are so central to national identity in the United States and Canada are tarnished by the large numbers of people within their borders who are without political or civil rights, and who have little prospect for obtaining those rights. These and other Western Hemisphere countries must find better ways to balance their interest in discouraging uninvited immigrants with the need and commitment to integrate newcomers into their societies.

For the Americas as a whole, migration can be managed effectively only if nations and governments face up to the fact that large-scale flows of people will mark hemispheric life for decades to come. Uncontrolled migration is already a source of growing tension in the Americas, and it may produce more open conflict in the future. Unilateral approaches to deter unwanted migration flows will only aggravate these tensions. With cooperative and jointly formulated policies that address the needs of sending and receiving societies and of the migrants themselves, migration can enrich every nation of the Hemisphere— and bind us all closer together.

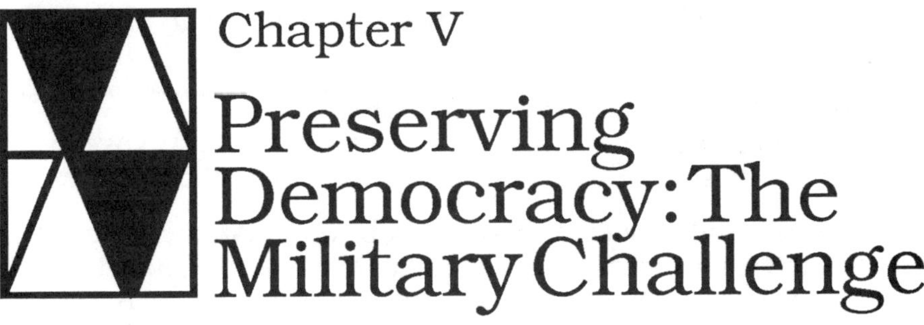

Chapter V

Preserving Democracy:The Military Challenge

After two decades of military rule, most of Latin America has restored constitutional democracy during the 1980s. Civilian governments have replaced military regimes in six countries of South America: Argentina, Brazil, Bolivia, Ecuador, Peru and Uruguay. Only two South American countries, Chile and Paraguay, still suffer military dictatorships. Even in Central America, where army rule has usually prevailed, civilian presidents now hold office, if not always full power, in every nation. Panama faces a major crisis as its people seek to shake off a military-dominated regime.

Latin America's region-wide turn toward democracy allows the people of the Hemisphere to enjoy the fruits of hard-won gains: freedom of expression and assembly, the right to participate in choosing governments and policies, and the effective protection of fundamental human rights.

Yet the new democracies of Latin America are far from robust. They are threatened by the region's crushing economic crisis, which limits their ability to meet public demands. They are enfeebled by the weakness of political institutions, which often aggravate political divisions instead of moderating and resolving conflicts.

And they are menaced by an old enemy: the danger of military intervention in politics. The 1988 political crisis in Panama dramatically illustrates that threat in a very special form, but the problem is widespread. Civil-military tensions exist in virtually every country of Latin America, and the current deterrents to military intervention do not provide adequate guarantees for the future. *Unless new patterns of civil-military relations can be firmly established, a new round of military coups may well occur in Latin America during the 1990s.*

Current Civil-Military Relations

Conflicts between Latin America's new civilian governments and the armed forces have focused on three issues:

- First, military establishments have resisted efforts by civilian leaders to curb their authority and reduce their privileges. During his first three years in office, Argentine President Raúl Alfonsin imposed a substantial degree of civilian control over the armed forces; military spending was cut and officers who spoke out in opposition on political matters were fired. The result, however, was intense military discontent. In Peru, too, President Alán Garcia had to buck strong military opposition to create a single Ministry of Defense, replacing the three traditional ministries of the Army, Navy and Air Force. His insistence on this reform produced a tense confrontation between the civilian government and the armed forces hierarchy, the dismissal of the air force commander, and considerable erosion of military support for the regime.

- Second, thorny conflicts have emerged every time a civilian regime has attempted to prosecute military officers accused of human rights violations. In countries plagued by insurgency, where torture and "disappearances" become common, the military demand for amnesty clashes with strong civilian calls for punishment and a visible reaffirmation of the rule of law. Junior officers in Argentina, many of whom felt threatened by the Alfonsin government's commitment to bring to trial those accused of human rights violations, revolted in April 1987, demanding public vindication of the anti-guerrilla operations they conducted during the "dirty war" of the mid-1970s. President Alfonsin was compelled to yield, and to propose a new law exempting active duty officers who acted under orders from prosecution for alleged offenses dating from that period. In Uruguay, after a year of political negotiations and military pressures, Congress approved President

Jorge Sanguinetti's proposal of amnesty for all officers accused of human rights abuses, but opposition parties succeeded in forcing a national referendum on the issue. In Peru, Haiti, El Salvador, and Guatemala—where most of the human rights violations attributed to military officers have gone unpunished—civilian leaders face a dilemma: prosecution in such cases causes dangerous friction with the armed forces, but failure to prosecute undermines the legitimacy of weak democratic regimes.

● Third, civil-military tensions have emerged over how to deal with guerrilla insurgencies in Colombia, El Salvador, Guatemala, and Peru. Whenever such uprisings threaten national security, conflicts are bound to arise over how to counter the threat. Violations of human rights committed in the anti-guerrilla struggle are particularly controversial.

These unresolved conflicts have fed pressures within the armed forces of Latin America to place limits on civilian authority or even to assert power directly. But there are counter-pressures as well. Military officers are painfully aware of the damage done to the armed forces as an institution during previous periods of military rule. The armed forces faced internal divisions, high officials became involved in corruption in some countries, and public support for the military declined sharply. In Argentina, the military regime suffered a humiliating defeat in the Malvinas/Falklands war with Great Britain. In Uruguay, the armed forces found their draft constitution rejected in a national plebiscite.

Such negative experiences should help deter military intervention in some cases, but not in all. In Brazil, El Salvador, Guatemala, and Peru, for example, public attitudes toward the military are not uniformly unfavorable, and the armed forces themselves are generally proud of their accomplishments. Many officers are confident that the military would be welcomed back to power. Military self-restraint alone cannot be counted on to prevent new challenges to civilian rule.

A second barrier to military intervention is public opinion. Military takeovers in Latin America have rarely succeeded without strong civilian backing. Across most sectors of society, civilians today squarely oppose a return to military rule. In Argentina, for instance, the April 1987 revolt was met by massive civilian demonstrations in defense of the democratic regime. So long as civilian presidents retain popular support and opposition leaders work within the constitutional system, the risk of military intervention is small. But the possible growth of civilian support for a resumption of military rule cannot be ignored, particularly in countries where prolonged economic deprivation is undermining the credibility of democratic governments.

International opposition can also play a role in dissuading military intervention. U.S. support for constitutional governments helped to prevent coups in Bolivia, Ecuador, El Salvador, and Honduras. Latin American and Western European democracies have contributed to shaping an international environment in the late 1980s that most Latin American officers recognize as adverse to military governments.

Fresh memories of the costs of direct military rule, the lack of civilian support for military takeovers, and international pressure have all helped deter military intervention during the 1980s. But this respite may not last; hazards to civilian rule continue.

- In Argentina, acts of military insubordination recur with some frequency. The Army is internally divided and alienated from civil society and the democratic regime.

- Ecuador has experienced two military revolts since 1985. Repeated confrontations between the President and Congress pose the risk of military intervention to arbitrate conflicts between the government and the opposition.

- In Peru, as a result of the Sendero Luminoso insurgency, large sections of the country are under *de facto* military rule. If guerrilla violence increases further, military and police repression may grow— with or without a return to direct military rule.

- In Brazil, the armed forces remain vocal on a wide range of issues, including many that are decidedly non-military. The country's intelligence services and its National Security Council are controlled by the armed forces. Thus far, the Constitutional Assembly has not agreed to proposals which would limit the traditionally broad mandate of the military to maintain internal order.

- In Uruguay, the armed forces and the civilian leadership have tried to reduce civil-military tensions, yet deep conflicts remain. Military writings continue to stress militant anti-communism and preparation for wars of "subversion". The armed forces continue to define their role as the ultimate guardians of public order.

- In El Salvador, Guatemala and Honduras, most officers have accepted civilian rule, partly to obtain U.S. military and economic aid. But their tolerance of civilian government is contingent upon *de facto* power-sharing in key policy decisions and, in some cases, upon a very high level of military autonomy.

- Haiti has inaugurated a civilian government, but only after a violent disruption of the election in November 1987 and the withdrawal of the leading candidates from the rescheduled election held in January 1988. By preventing the first election and deciding the outcome of the second, Haiti's armed forces left the newly-installed government with scant legitimacy, domestic or international.

- In Panama, a civilian president inaugurated in 1984 after 16 years of direct military rule was forced from office a year later. The civilian vice-president, who then assumed the presidency in a military-dominated regime, was deposed in early 1987 by the head of

Panama's defense forces, General Noriega. A severe crisis has ensued: U.S. economic sanctions have brought the country's economy to a standstill; the military-controlled regime cannot govern; and the opposition is unable to dislodge the military.

- In Chile, the 1980 Constitution imposed by General Augusto Pinochét established a plebiscite in 1988 or 1989 on the presidential candidate nominated by the current Military Junta, presumably the General himself. Even if Pinochét were to lose a bid to prolong his 14-year presidency, the 1980 Constitution assures a permanent political role for the armed forces in government.

Most Latin American officers today would prefer to avoid direct military rule, but traditional views of the military's role in politics still prevail. Most officers see the armed forces as the ultimate guardians of national interests and guarantors of national security. Their lack of full confidence in civilian leadership makes it difficult for them to accept a fundamental principle of constitutional democracy: that military power should be subordinate to civilian authority.

Reducing the Long-Term Risk of Military Intervention

To lower the risk of military interventions, civilian governments must be strengthened. Democratic leaders must enhance the legitimacy of constitutional authority. Civilians must resolve political conflicts without recourse to potential allies in the military. When democratic regimes permit civil conflict and political violence to erupt, the armed forces are inevitably drawn back toward politics.

How military officers think about their role in politics is deeply affected by their assessment of how well civilian regimes perform. Civilian control will not last when military officers view political leaders as ineffective, corrupt, or influenced by "subversive" ideologies. If civilians cannot be counted upon to govern in the "national interest" or to protect "national security", leaders of the armed forces feel they must assume the role of political guardian. This guardianship role seems natural when the military see themselves as better trained and organized than civilian political leaders. Such views are common in the armed forces of Brazil, Peru, and Central America.

The experience to date of Latin America's new democracies highlights three major areas of concern.

First, in many countries, civilian political institutions are still relatively fragile, in part because their growth has been stunted by prior coups and military governments. Legislatures and local governments are underdeveloped and under-funded. Most political parties are feeble, with scant voice in the policy process. The proliferation of parties makes it hard to hold them accountable to the electorate. Fragmented party systems produce personalist or minority governments with unstable bases of support.

Weak political institutions are particularly vulnerable in countries with powerful, well-organized militaries. Stable civilian regimes have emerged in countries—such as Colombia, Mexico, and Venezuela today, or Chile and Uruguay in earlier periods—that developed strong civilian institutions and traditions *prior* to the development of modern military forces. Unless parties, legislatures, and the courts are strengthened, the imbalances in organizational effectiveness between these and the armed forces puts at risk civilian authority over the military.

Second, the hemispheric economic crisis of the 1980s has frustrated efforts to strengthen democratic politics. Far from meeting the needs of their citizens for jobs, income and services, civilian governments have had to embrace austerity in order to pay debts inherited from their (often military) predecessors. Inflation and cuts in social services have eroded the living standard of most Latin Americans. Declining real incomes, unemployment, increasing gaps between rich and poor, and worsening crime and corruption: all plague the constitutional democracies.

Third, in a number of countries, the armed forces still maintain a strong voice on non-military policies. In Brazil, six of the twenty-six members of the cabinet are active-duty generals or admirals. In El Salvador, Guatemala, and Honduras, the military retain an implicit veto power; in Panama, and perhaps in Haiti, military leaders govern within formally civilian regimes. When military pressures force civilian authorities to serve interests and values in conflict with those dominant in civilian society, the elected government inevitably loses some of its legitimacy. The political histories of Argentina and Brazil show that such "limited democracies" are inherently unstable. The public tends not to accept such regimes as fully legitimate, and they are consequently more vulnerable to renewed military intervention.

Military Policy and Military Reform

Reducing the risk of new coups is not just a matter of improving the performance of civilian governments. It also requires a concerted effort to redefine the relationship of those governments to the armed forces. National government must have the authority to make foreign and defense policy, establish military budgets and force levels, and set the rules that govern the armed forces and their relations with the rest of the state and society. In Latin America today, only Colombia, Costa Rica, Mexico, and Venezuela have established fully effective systems of civilian control. In the rest of the region, civilian presidents and legislatures have formal but not full authority over the armed forces.

Civilian deference to military demands has been defended as the only "politically realistic" alternative for fragile democratic governments. Yet the absence of strong civilian control perpetuates civil-military conflicts and thus undermines the stability of Latin American democracies.

Military autonomy from civilian control, for instance, leaves military education in the hands of the armed forces. Despite the transition to civilian rule, the political content of military education has remained virtually unchanged. Military curricula mostly continue to emphasize the hard-line anti-communist world view of the 1960s, stressing internal subversion as the principal threat to national security. In countries not faced with active insurgencies, civilian presidents rarely share the military's preoccupation with internal security. Many officers, in turn, question the commitment of civilian politicians to protecting national defense.

The gulf that often exists between the views of military and civilian leaders has not been successfully bridged, thus allowing scope for a military perception of civilian policies as "contrary to national interests." Despite civilian repudiation of the excesses and abuses sometimes caused by the "national security doctrines" of the 1960s and 1970s, military schools still define national security to include a wide range of political, socioeconomic, and international factors. Policy decisions which normally are reserved to civilian authority in the United States or Europe are viewed in Latin America as having military implications. Accordingly, officers feel their views should count heavily.

Military officers and civilian leaders may also have different concepts of democracy and the political process. In military writings, democracy is sometimes idealized as a "way of life", rather than understood as a set of institutions and norms for self-government, policy-making, and conflict management. Until military officers think of democracy in terms of procedures to be safeguarded at almost any cost, the chances of military intervention will remain high.

Democratic governments in Latin America must develop strategies for changing the attitudes of military officers about their proper political role and integrating the armed forces more successfully within the democratic regime. Democratic governments must design and implement a *military policy* to create the conditions for civilian control.

Such a policy must be more than an attempt to reduce military privileges or restrict military autonomy. It must strive to produce fundamental changes in military thinking—regarding internal security and subversion, the view of the military as the guardian and embodiment of national values, and the belief that national security embraces all aspects of national policy. *Lasting changes in civil-military relations require basic shifts in the attitudes of Latin America's officers.*

Constructing a Democratic Model of Civil-Military Relations

A long-term policy for civilian control is essential to integrate the armed forces into Latin America's democracies. The starting point for defining such a policy should be sustained dialogues among political leaders, civilian experts, and retired and active duty military officers. The setting, auspices, and timing for such dialogues should vary from country-to-country, but they should all face some common questions: the mission of the armed forces and the scope of its mandate; the level of resources that should be allocated to the military; the appropriate relation between military officers and civilian authorities on national security questions; and the nature and content of military education.

Such civil-military dialogues would be unprecedented in most countries. Civilians have traditionally neglected such questions; even today, most civilians tend to define the military's role primarily in negative terms—what the military should not do—rather than specify the positive missions the armed forces should perform. Military officers, in turn, rarely discuss important issues with civilians; they are usually set apart from civil society.

Forging a stable relationship between the armed forces and democratic societies will require attention to improving the process of civil-military interaction. Public and private forums must be established in order to encourage exchanges among civilian and military leaders from a broad spectrum of opinion.

Dialogue by itself will not resolve basic civil-military conflicts, of course. Exchanges of opinion among military and civilian leaders is surely not enough to produce a new model of civil-military relations. Yet it would be equally naive to think that such a model can be devised by civilian leaders alone. The first step is to begin sustained and constructive communication.

A parallel step must be to strengthen democratic institutions. Without improvements in governmental capacity for policy-making and conflict management, civilian control of the military will remain a utopian aspiration. The persistent institutional imbalances between the armed forces and civil society need to be overcome— not primarily by weakening the armed forces but rather by bolstering civilian institutions. Civilian leaders themselves have a fundamental obligation to abide by constitutional principles and the rule of law. Civilians cannot expect the armed forces to observe standards of public morality or constitutional norms which they themselves violate.

The Hemisphere's democratic governments must consistently express support for constitutional democracy. International pressure is needed to promote democratic change in Chile, Haiti, Panama, and Paraguay—and in Cuba and Nicaragua. In the case of Panama, diplomatic pressures for democratization should be multilateral, with full assurances that opposition to the Noriega dictatorship will not affect compliance with the terms of the Panama Canal treaties. In the case of Haiti, democratic countries should oppose efforts by the armed forces to turn the new civilian government into a facade for military control. In Chile, democratic countries must oppose both Pinochét's attempt to perpetuate himself in office and the continuing political role for the military established in the 1980 constitution. If those constitutional provisions are not altered, Chile's government will be neither truly civilian nor democratic even after Pinochét.

Economic support for democratic governments is badly needed from the United States, Japan, and other industrialized nations. The legitimacy of civilian regimes in Latin America rests in part on their ability to manage their economic problems and satisfy socio-economic demands unmet by previous regimes. So long as democratic governments are forced to deepen the austerity measures imposed by previous military governments, popular support for democracy will surely diminish. *If economic crisis destroys confidence in civilian rule, the armed forces will once again be drawn to center stage.*

Finally, both the United States and Latin American governments should analyze the political consequences of military aid and training programs. U.S. officials often claim that these programs help instill respect for democracy and human rights. This may sometimes be the case, but the United States has trained over 100,000 Latin

American officers and soldiers since 1950. The record of military coups during the past 35 years suggests that the training programs have not succeeded in ingraining desirable norms about military intervention in politics. Most U.S. courses are, in fact, technical, but some may contribute to civil-military tensions. For example, the concerns of Latin American officers over "indirect aggression and communist subversion" may be reinforced by training which reflects the attention given by the United States to Soviet power and policy, a preoccupation which few civilian governments in Latin America fully share.

In countries with weak civilian institutions, U.S. military aid programs may inadvertently aggravate the imbalances in organizational effectiveness between civilian and military institutions. In Central America, military assistance programs have contributed to the development of military forces that are more technically sophisticated and better organized than civilian institutions. In the Caribbean, U.S. attempts to strengthen local security forces may create similar imbalances in societies where civilian dominance is fragile. Advantages in funding and training may reinforce the latent belief among some officers that they are more qualified to govern than civilian political leaders.

U.S. military training programs should therefore be provided only to countries where there are demonstrated mutual security interests, and where military assistance will not weaken democratic politics but rather help defend it from attack. Small-scale grants of military assistance may sometimes be warranted as symbolic expressions of U.S. support for democratic governments, but such grants should be extended cautiously, with due regard for their political impact.

Within existing U.S. military programs, greater efforts should be made to reinforce the message that constitutional democracy is vital for hemispheric security. In the past, these programs have often assumed that U.S. views on civilian control would be transferred automatically through exposure to the U.S. model. This assumption fails to recognize the depth and difficulty of the problem. Democratic concepts and the importance of civilian control should be actively promoted, both in formal training and in the foreign trainee information programs. The recent and welcome efforts by officials of the Department of State and the U.S. Southern Command to disseminate policy statements on democracy in Latin America should be strongly reinforced, for instance.

Canada and the Scandinavian countries may well provide more relevant role models for the Latin American militaries than does the United States. Western European nations should be prepared to play a greater role as suppliers of military training in Latin America, as they have already in the areas of arms sales and co-production agreements. Small-scale European military aid programs would expose Latin American countries to alternative forms of civilian control.

Finally, European nations, Canada, and the United States should be ready to provide training programs for Latin American civilians involved in defense and military policy. A major obstacle to civilian control in Latin America is the scarcity of non-military personnel with expertise on security issues. Congressional staffs, presidential aides, ministry of defense officials, and academic experts need to understand security and defense questions. Only then will they be in a position to improve civilian oversight and assert control over military forces and intelligence agencies.

The Challenge

Establishing a durable and democratic system of civil-military relations is a long-term challenge. Meeting it will require innovative leadership and sustained effort to change military attitudes and broaden civil-military understanding. There are no quick or simple solutions to current civil-military tensions, nor are there easy ways to change deeply-rooted patterns of relations between the armed forces and civilian governments.

The Hemisphere's return to democracy in the 1980s provides Latin America with the opportunity to work toward civilian control over military establishments, and to integrate the armed forces into democratic societies. But that opportunity could prove to be short-lived. Unless a concerted effort is made now, the Hemisphere might lose its best chance ever to end a history of repeated military interventions.

Appendix A

Supplemental Comments of Dialogue Members

Peggy Antrobus

The chapter on debt accurately states that the debt burden "ultimately falls most heavily on the poor, particularly women and children," but it misses the key point that most current adjustment policies reflect an ideology that accords a subordinate role for women in the economy. These policies are especially exploitative of the time and energy of poor women. They also frustrate the achievement of the most important long-term goal of development: improving the welfare of the majority of the people. Second, current debt problems cannot be resolved without addressing the fundamental imbalances in economic and political relationships between the United States and Latin America. Issues of international trade and investment, for example, must be part of the debate on debt.

The migration chapter fails to consider adequately three important points: how racism affects the differential treatment of Cuban and Haitian migrants; the effect of U.S. policies toward Latin America and the Caribbean on migration flows; and the economic benefits to sending countries of migration. More liberal immigration policies by the United States and Canada should be viewed as a legitimate way to assist Latin American and Caribbean countries.

Nicolás Ardito Barletta

I do not believe that addictive drugs which have been proven to damage human health can be legalized. Even though all angles of a problem should be studied with a scientific approach, I think that far more is to be gained by increasing the national programs of demand and supply controls, and that inter-American cooperation is necessary to deal effectively with this truly hemispheric problem. I would underline the chapter's central message: The United States must increase its educational and other demand control programs, and the Latin American countries need to strengthen their efforts to control supply, in order to avoid, among other things, falling prey to control by bands of undesirables who will stop at nothing to get what they want.

Guillermo Bueso
I want to point out that it is not only in Honduras that civilian and military institutions are weak and subject to corruption; this problem affects every country of Central America. And Honduras, like the other countries, is struggling to overcome the problem.

Joan Ganz Cooney
This report illuminates the key issues in U.S.-Latin American relations and provides a needed and balanced perspective. Because of my responsibility as a member of the Board of the Chase Manhattan Bank, however, I must abstain from taking a position on Chapter II, except to say it thoughtfully discusses very complex issues about which reasonable people can differ.

Richard W. Fisher
I support this thoughtful and comprehensive statement on the changing agenda in U.S.-Latin American relations. In particular, I commend the attention paid to the important issue of strengthening civilian control of the military and fostering improved civil-military relations. I would urge that the United States political authorities encourage the U.S. military to resume its interrupted dialogue with the armed forces leadership in Latin America, especially in the countries of the Southern Cone. It is true that U.S. military training has not always successfully ingrained democratic values but that is no reason to abandon this effort; on the contrary, creative approaches to this challenge are needed and should be emphasized.

Florángela Gómez Ordoñez

I agree with most of the analysis and conclusions of this report. I cannot, however, endorse Chapter III, "Drugs: A Shared Tragedy," because it fails to reflect all the effort and sacrifices of the government and people of Colombia.

Xabier Gorostiaga

Although I welcome the Dialogue's strong support of the Esquipulas peace process, and its consistent opposition to military approaches in Central America, I believe this report is too Washington-oriented in suggesting that Nicaragua is the principal obstacle to peace and security in Central America. Indeed, independent observers throughout the Hemisphere agree that only Costa Rica and Nicaragua have made positive steps to implement the peace accords. The report fails to discuss adequately recent trends in El Salvador and Honduras or the serious crisis in Panama. Most important, it avoids sufficiently strong criticism of the U.S. Administration, even after the revelations of the "Iran-Contra" affair. The current U.S. Administration, not Nicaragua, has been and still is the principal obstacle to the implementation of the Esquipulas peace accords. This point is recognized by leading presidential candidates in the United States and by America's friends internationally, and it should be stated more forcefully by the Dialogue.

I do have some reservations about the chapter on Latin America's debt. Again, I find the analysis lucid and constructive, but believe the presentation is too Washington-focused; it puts too much confidence in the World Bank and the IMF; it does not take adequate account of the proposals by the U.N. Economic Commission for Latin America and the Caribbean (ECLAC) and of the Latin American Economic System (SELA); and it does not sufficiently emphasize the responsibility for the United States to put its own economic house in order.

Osvaldo Hurtado Larrea

The report's discussion of security in Central America does not sufficiently emphasize U.S. responsibility for the current situation or the commitments that the United States must now make if a lasting peace is to be achieved. The United States should be censured for its military intervention in violation of the principles and norms of international law.

With regard to civil-military relations, I would emphasize that the President of Ecuador, by frequently exceeding his constitutional authority, has increased the risk of military intervention in my country's politics.

Finally, in analyzing Latin America's economic problems, it is necessary to recognize that foreign corporations are no longer interested in investing in the region's economies despite the incentives provided by many countries.

Fernando Léniz

I want to express several reservations about the chapter on civil-military relations. The analysis does not give sufficient attention to the real security challenges to Latin America posed by the Soviet Union and its capacity to foment unrest. Nor does it adequately deal with the highly repressive regimes of Cuba and Nicaragua. It also fails to emphasize the grave dangers of guerilla insurgencies, particularly the activities of the Sendero Luminoso in Peru, and the importance for democracy of controlling those insurgencies.

I am also troubled by the suggestion that the 1980 constitution was imposed on the people of Chile. The majority of voters approved the constitution in a plebiscite. Moreover, international pressures on the Pinochét government are likely to be counter-productive; they will not help to advance democratic rule in Chile. This is best left to the Chilean people themselves, without outside interference.

The chapter on debt does not take sufficient account of the damage done by the extremely high interest rates of the early 1980s, which produced nearly one-quarter of the present debt. U.S. economic policies were mainly responsible for this sharp rise in interest. It is also important to recognize that the easy-lending policies of commercial banks resulted in many bad loans, for which the banks themselves should assume responsibility.

Charles McC. Mathias

The chapter on the debt crisis accurately evaluates the problem. It also recognizes the uncertainties that compound the difficulties such as Congressional attitudes toward another contribution to the World Bank and commercial banking attitudes toward further private credit. It is not realistic, therefore, to call for consensus for "accelerated lending" by international financial institutions and for expanded lending by commercial banks without addressing the pre-conditions for such initiatives.

José Francisco Peña Gómez

Many parts of this report are excellent, especially the balanced and informative discussions of debt and drugs and the emphasis on supporting the Esquipulas approach in Central America. I am troubled, however, by two sections in the report, which seem to reflect a North American bias. I believe the treatment of Panama is unfair, and especially think that referring to the indictment of General Noriega in the United States does not help resolve Panama's serious crisis. Similarly, I believe the discussion of Central America's security problems is unbalanced in implying that Nicaragua and Cuba are responsible for this region's insecurity and failing to emphasize sufficiently the serious responsibility of the United States and the Contras.

John Petty

The Dialogue's report is a thoughtful and constructive analysis with positive recommendations on a broad range of issues. While I support the report's main approaches, it has not been appropriate for me, as newly-named Chairman of the Inter-American Development Bank's High Level Review Committee, to participate in the conclusions.

Augusto Ramírez Ocampo

I strongly commend this excellent report, although I am not fully in accord with all of the conclusions in the chapters on armed forces and democracy, on drug trafficking, and on Central America.

I agree that strengthening Latin American democracy requires that both the armed forces and civilian governments assume their proper roles. The chapter, however, does not sufficiently emphasize that the armed forces and civilian governments have very different areas of responsibility, and that these must be mutually respected, as has been the tradition in Colombia. Moreover, there may be a risk in civil-military dialogues, which, despite their intent, could themselves give rise to interventions against the independent operation of democratic government.

As the report states, the drug problem requires combined action by both the producing and consumer nations, with a particular emphasis on reducing demand. To blame drug-producing nations, withhold aid from them, or set strict conditions for such aid could lead to confrontations between governments with shared goals. I do not, however, concur with all of the statements made in the chapter. For instance, according to the information I have, it is inaccurate to say that Colombia has more cocaine addicts per capita than the United States.

Regarding Central America, I would more strongly emphasize the role of the Contadora group in creating a framework for resolving the crisis. Now that the five Central American presidents have taken their own initiative for peace and development, the United States and the Soviet Union should accept their obligation to promote this initiative. The peace process is advancing and deserves the support of the entire international community. The Sapoá agreement represents a triumph of negotiating strategy over military force, as well as a hope for peace. I would also call attention to the work of the United Nations in developing a "Special Plan for Economic Cooperation for Central America." This plan, which I am coordinating as the Special Representative of the Secretary General, has been developed in close consultation with the region's governments and emphasizes the interdependence of peace and development.

Brent Scowcroft
There is much to commend in this report. The analysis

is thorough and the recommendations by and large are thoughtful. Yet I find the underlying tone troubling.

Although I recognize the difficulties of establishing genuine inter-American give and take, I believe the report, broadly speaking, tends to absolve Latin American countries from responsibility for the problems addressed. The debt chapter emphasizes that the Baker plan has not produced the resources it promised and minimizes the failure of Latin American countries to deliver on their obligations for reform. The narcotics chapter down-plays the responsibility of Latin American countries for dealing with supply, criticizing "counter-productive pressure" on them.

The chapter on the armed forces is mostly on the mark, but too much of the burden is placed on the Latin American military. Certainly significant responsibility rests there, but the report makes light of the feeling of the Latin American military that they are the true guardians of the state. Military frustrations with the ineptitude and pettiness of many civilian governments are glossed over. The statement that U.S. training programs have not succeeded in ingraining norms about democracy in the Latin American military I believe to be gratuitous and misleading. The migration chapter is relatively well-balanced, but there is greater emphasis on the duties of the receiving countries (i.e., the United States) than on the responsibilities of sending countries to devise measures to make their citizens want to remain at home.

The chapter on Central America is the most troubling. The report states that the Dialogue has consistently opposed military approaches, yet ignores the fact that the guerrillas in El Salvador and the Sandinista government in Nicaragua initiated and continue to perpetuate the violence. The report also ignores the role of the Contras in bringing the Sandinistas to the bargaining table. By contending that the United States should restrict its Contra aid to "genuinely humanitarian assistance," it would remove pressure on the Sandinistas at the very moment it is beginning to bear fruit. This refusal to accept reality in Central America is one of the report's most serious flaws. These comments and objections notwithstanding, the report represents a useful contribution to the dialogue in an area of critical importance to the United States.

Peter Tarnoff

I have several reservations. Regarding the chapter on narcotics, I would not exclude U.S. pressure and sanctions against drug-producing and trafficking countries as the text seems to recommend. Furthermore, I would oppose having the Inter-American Dialogue study the legalization of any illicit drug, which is a complicated, controversial and primarily domestic American issue. Personally, I am against any such legalization.

I do not believe that the United States should negotiate directly with Nicaragua on questions of the Central American military balance. Such issues should be resolved primarily by the signers of the Guatemala Accord, although the United States and the Soviet Union might also usefully exchange views on the subject.

I find unconvincing the references to the insufficiencies of past U.S. military and training programs. I do agree that such programs should place greater emphasis on helping the military play a constructive role in representative civilian regimes.

The chapter on migration seems to me to seriously underestimate the difficulties involved in obtaining a regulated and predictable flow of immigrants from Latin America to the United States. Moreover, I do not feel comfortable urging foreign governments to step up their interventions on behalf of migrant rights in this country. It also strikes me as prejudicial to U.S. interests worldwide for the United States to increase its immigration quota from Mexico. Such exceptional treatment would provoke heavy pressure for expanded quotas elsewhere.

Cyrus Vance

I warmly endorse much of this report, particularly its constructive approach to Central America and to the important issue of civil-military relations.

I have two serious reservations, however. First, I cannot subscribe to all the eight statements of consensus listed on pages 37 through 39 of the chapter on Latin America's debt crisis. I particularly disagree with the recommendation that the commercial banks should provide "substantially more capital" to the debtor nations; indeed, this recommendation contradicts the persuasive analysis earlier in the same chapter about why the banks must limit further lending at this stage. Second, I must disassociate myself from Chapter III; I feel strongly that it fails to address adequately the very serious issue of drugs or to offer practical solutions to this difficult problem.

Appendix B

Participants in the Inter-American Dialogue

From the United States and Canada:

Sol M. Linowitz (Co-Chairman)

Sol M. Linowitz is senior counsel of the international law firm of Coudert Brothers. He served as President Carter's personal representative for the Middle East Peace Negotiations and as co-negotiator for the Panama Canal Treaties. In the mid-1970s, he was Chairman of the Commission on U.S.-Latin American relations. From 1966 to 1969, he was U.S. Ambassador to the Organization of American States. Previously, he had been Chairman of Xerox.

Peter D. Bell (Co-Vice Chairman)

Peter D. Bell is President of the Edna McConnell Clark Foundation. He was senior associate of the Carnegie Endowment for International Peace from 1984 to 1986, and President of the Inter-American Foundation from 1980 to 1983. He is Chairman of the Board of the Refugee Policy Group and a member of the boards of the Institute of the Americas, the World Peace Foundation, and Americas Watch.

Bruce Babbitt

Bruce Babbitt was a candidate for the presidential nomination of the Democratic Party in 1988. He was Governor of Arizona from 1978 to 1986, and served previously as Arizona's Attorney General. He also has been Co-Chairman of the Democratic Leadership Council and Chairman of the Democratic Governors' Association. Governor

Babbitt served on the President's Commission on the Accident of Three Mile Island, and was Chairman of the Nuclear Safety Oversight Committee.

Michael D. Barnes

Michael D. Barnes is a partner at the Washington, D.C. law firm of Arent, Fox, Kintner, Plotkin & Kahn. From 1979 to 1987, he was a Member from Maryland of the U. S. House of Representatives and served as Chairman of the Subcommittee on Western Hemisphere Affairs of the Committee on Foreign Affairs. Mr. Barnes is on the boards of the U.S. Committee for UNICEF, the Overseas Development Council, the International Human Rights Law Group, and the Center for National Policy, among others.

James F. Beré

James F. Beré is Chairman and Chief Executive Officer of Borg-Warner Corporation. He is a member and former Chairman of the Advisory Council on Japan-U.S. Economic Relations, a director of the Chicago Council on Foreign Relations, and a trustee of the Committee on Economic Development. Mr. Beré is also Vice Chairman of the Board of the Chicago Museum of Science and Technology.

Thornton F. Bradshaw

Thornton F. Bradshaw is a consultant for General Electric. He has served as Chairman of the Board of RCA Corporation and as President of Atlantic Richfield. He is a member of the boards of Atlantic Richfield, Champion International, First Boston Corporation, the MacArthur Foundation, the Rockefeller Brothers Fund, the Institute for Advanced Study at Princeton, and the Aspen Institute.

McGeorge Bundy

McGeorge Bundy, Professor of History at New York University, was President of the Ford Foundation from 1966 to 1979. From 1961 until 1966, he was Special Assistant to the President for National Security Affairs. Previously, he was Dean of the Faculty of Arts and Sciences at Harvard University.

Terence C. Canavan

Terence C. Canavan is Executive Vice President of Chemical Bank and heads the Latin American Division of its World Banking Group. He served as Director of the Bank's affiliate in Caracas from 1973 to 1976, and previously represented the Bank in Mexico City and Madrid.

Joan Ganz Cooney

Joan Ganz Cooney has been President of Children's Television Workshop since 1980. She serves on the boards of several corporations, including Xerox, Chase Manhattan, and Johnson and Johnson.

Ralph P. Davidson

Ralph P. Davidson is President of the Kennedy Center in Washington, D.C. Previously, he was Chairman of the Board of Time, Inc. and Publisher of *Time*. He is a member of the President's Commission on Executive Exchange and the President's Commission on International Youth Exchange. He serves on the board of the National Urban League, the Committee for Economic Development, Allied-Signal, and ITT.

Jorge I. Domínguez

Jorge I. Domínguez is Professor of Government at Harvard University and is former President of the Latin American Studies Association. Dr. Domínguez, the author of numerous books and articles, is one of the foremost authorities in the United States on his native Cuba. He was series editor for the Public Broadcasting System's four documentaries on Central America and Cuba, shown in April 1985.

Marie-Josée Drouin

Marie-Josée Drouin is Executive Director of the Hudson Institute in Canada. An economist and public policy analyst, she has directed studies on economic, social, and political issues in Canada. She is a member of several corporate boards, and the boards of the Canadian Center for Arms Control and Disarmament and of the University of Quebec Foundation.

Antonio Luis Ferré

Antonio Luis Ferré is President of *El Nuevo Día*, one of Puerto Rico's major daily newspapers. Mr. Ferré was appointed regional President for Puerto Rico of the National Alliance of Businessmen by President Ford. He is Vice Chairman of the Board of the Banco de Ponce, and a member of the boards of American Airlines, the American Newspaper Publishers' Association, and the Metropolitan Life Insurance Company.

Maurice A. Ferré

Maurice A. Ferré, now a business consultant, served six terms as Mayor of Miami. He was the first National Chairman of the Hispanic Council on Foreign Affairs, and a member of President Ford's Immigration Commission and President Carter's Commission on Ambassadorial Appointments.

Richard W. Fisher

Richard W. Fisher is Managing Partner of Fisher Capital Management of Dallas and Chairman of the Board of the Institute of the Americas. From 1977 to 1979, he served as Executive Assistant to the Secretary of the Treasury. Mr. Fisher serves on numerous boards and committees, including the visiting committees of Harvard University's Center for Science and Advanced International Affairs and of Johns Hopkins University's School of International Studies, and the nominating committee of the Council on Foreign Relations.

Albert Fishlow

Albert Fishlow is Chairman of the Department of Economics at the University of California at Berkeley. From 1978 to 1982, he was Director of the Concilium on International and Area Studies at Yale University. In 1975 and 1976, he served as Deputy Assistant Secretary of State for Inter-American Affairs. Dr. Fishlow, an authority on Brazil and on international financial issues, has written many books and articles.

Douglas A. Fraser

Douglas A. Fraser is the former President of the United

Auto Workers. He is currently University Professor of Labor Studies at Wayne State University in Detroit.

Andrew J. Goodpaster

Andrew J. Goodpaster, General, U.S. Army (Ret.) served as Superintendent of the U.S. Military Academy at West Point from 1977 to 1981 and was Supreme Commander of Allied Forces in Europe from 1969 to 1974. He is Chairman of the American Battle Monuments Commission and Chairman of the Atlantic Council of the United States. General Goodpaster has also been the President of the Institute for Defense Analysis.

Hanna Holborn Gray

Hanna Holborn Gray has been President of the University of Chicago since 1978. She has also served as President of Yale University, Provost of Yale University, and Dean of the College of Arts and Sciences at Northwestern University. She is a member of the boards of Morgan Guaranty Trust, J.P. Morgan, Atlantic Richfield, and other corporations.

David A. Hamburg

David A. Hamburg has been President of the Carnegie Corporation of New York since 1983. He has served as President and Chairman of the Board of the American Association for the Advancement of Science and President of the Institute of Medicine of the National Academy of Sciences. He has also been Chairman of the Department of Psychiatry at Stanford University, and has served on the Board of Trustees of the Rockefeller University and Mt. Sinai Medical Center.

Ivan L. Head

Ivan L. Head has been President of the International Development Research Centre of Canada since 1978. From 1968 to 1978, he was Special Assistant to the Prime Minister, with responsibility for foreign policy and the conduct of international relations. He served abroad as a Foreign Service Officer and has been a professor of international law. He is a member of the Independent Commission on International Humanitarian Issues.

Theodore M. Hesburgh

Theodore M. Hesburgh, C.S.C., is President Emeritus of the University of Notre Dame, where he served as President from 1952 to 1987. He has been Chairman of the boards of the Rockefeller Foundation, the Overseas Development Council, the U.S. Commission on Civil Rights, and the Select Commission on Immigration. Father Hesburgh has received more honorary degrees than any other individual in the United States.

Don Johnston

Don Johnston is former Chairman and Chief Executive Officer of J. Walter Thompson Company, the oldest advertising company in the United States. He has been Chairman of the American Association of Advertising Agencies and a director of the Advertising Council and the Advertising Educational Foundation.

Juanita M. Kreps

Juanita M. Kreps is Vice President Emeritus of Duke University. From 1977 to 1979, she was U.S. Secretary of Commerce. Dr. Kreps has been a professor, a writer, and an administrator. She currently serves on the boards of Citicorp, R.J. Reynolds, AT&T, and United Airlines.

Charles McC. Mathias, Jr.

Charles McC. Mathias, Jr. is a partner at the law firm of Jones, Day, Reavis and Pogue. From 1968 to 1987, he was United States Senator from Maryland, and earlier served four terms as a Member of the House of Representatives. In 1985, Senator Mathias was elected President of the North Atlantic Assembly.

Robert S. McNamara

Robert S. McNamara served from 1968 to 1981 as President of the World Bank. From 1961 to 1968, he was U.S. Secretary of Defense. He has also been President of the Ford Motor Company. Mr. McNamara serves on numerous boards, including the Bank of America, the Ford Foundation, the Brookings Institution, and the Aspen Institute.

A. Roy Megarry

A. Roy Megarry is Publisher of *The Globe and Mail*, Canada's largest national newspaper. Previously, Mr. Megarry served as Vice President of Torstar, a communications conglomerate, and Director of Toronto Star Newspapers Limited. Mr. Megarry is a frequent speaker and writer on Third World issues.

William G. Milliken

William G. Milliken was Michigan's longest serving Governor, occupying the position from 1969 to 1982. He has been Chairman of the National Governors' Association and the Republican Governors' Conference. A former business executive, Mr. Milliken serves on the boards of Burroughs Corporation, Chrysler Corporation, and the Ford Foundation. He is Chairman of the Center for the Great Lakes.

Edmund S. Muskie

Edmund S. Muskie is a senior partner of the international law firm Chadbourne and Parke. He was Secretary of State from 1980 to 1981, Senator from Maine from 1958 to 1980, and Governor of Maine from 1954 to 1958.

John R. Petty

John R. Petty is Chairman of Marine Midland Bank, Inc. He was a Partner and Director of Lehman Brothers, Kuhn and Loeb from 1972 to 1976, and Assistant Secretary of the Treasury from 1968 to 1972. He is President of the Foreign Bondholders Protection Council and a member of the boards of NBC, RCA and other corporations.

Ralph A. Pfeiffer, Jr.

Ralph A. Pfeiffer, Jr. was the Chairman and Chief Operating Officer of IBM World Trade Americas/Far East Corporation and Senior Vice President of IBM. He serves on many boards, including the International Chamber of Commerce, the Center for Strategic and International Studies, the Royal Bank of Canada and SmithKline Beckman Corporation. Mr. Pfeiffer has been Chairman of the Independent College Fund of America.

Robert D. Ray

Robert D. Ray is President and Chief Executive Officer of Life Investors, Inc. He was Governor of Iowa from 1969 until 1983, and has been a Republican Party leader at both national and state levels. Mr. Ray was U.S. Delegate to the United Nations General Assembly in 1984, and is Chairman of the Indo-Chinese Refugee Panel.

Elliot L. Richardson

Elliot L. Richardson is a senior partner of the law firm Milbank, Tweed, Hadley, and McCloy in Washington, D.C. He has served as Attorney General, Secretary of Defense, Secretary of Commerce, Secretary of Health, Education and Welfare, Deputy Secretary of State, Ambassador to the Court of Saint James's, and U.S. Representative to the Law of the Sea Conference.

Brent Scowcroft

Brent Scowcroft was Assistant to the President for National Security Affairs from 1975 to 1977. He is now a consultant on international affairs and Vice Chairman of Kissinger Associates, Inc. A retired Lieutenant General of the U.S. Air Force, he is Vice Chairman of the U.S. United Nations Association and a director of the Council on Foreign Relations and of the Atlantic Council. In 1983, General Scowcroft chaired the President's Commission on Strategic Forces.

Paula Stern

Paula Stern is a senior associate of the Carnegie Endowment for International Peace. From 1978 to 1986, she served as a member of the U.S. International Trade Commission, for the last two years as its Chairwoman. Ms. Stern serves on several boards, including the Carnegie Council on Ethics and International Affairs and Scott Paper Company.

Peter Tarnoff

Peter Tarnoff has been President of the Council on Foreign Relations in New York since 1986. Previously, Mr. Tarnoff was Executive Director of the World Affairs Council

Alberto Quirós C. and Fernando Léniz

Sol Linowitz and John R. Petty

Nicolás Ardito Barletta and Jesús Silva Herzog

Albert Fishlow, Fernando Henrique Cardoso, José María Dagnino
Pastore, Celso Lafer, and Peter Hakim

Peggy Antrobus and Oliver Clarke

Rodrigo Botero and Anthony Solomon

Xabier Gorostiaga

Robert S. McNamara

110

Elliot L. Richardson

Alejandro Foxley

of Northern California and President of the International Advisory Corporation in San Francisco. From 1977 until 1981, Mr. Tarnoff was Executive Secretary of the Department of State and has served as Special Assistant to Secretaries of State Edmund Muskie and Cyrus Vance.

Cyrus R. Vance

Cyrus R. Vance is a senior partner of the New York law firm Simpson, Thacher and Bartlett. From 1977 to 1980, he was Secretary of State. He was previously Secretary of the Army and the Defense Department's General Counsel. He serves on several corporate boards, including Manufacturers Hanover Trust, IBM, U.S. Steel, and the New York Times.

Clifton R. Wharton, Jr.

Clifton R. Wharton, Jr. is the President and Chief Executive Officer of TIAA/CREF. He previously served as Chancellor of the State University of New York System, President of Michigan State University, and Chairman of the Board of the Rockefeller Foundation. Mr. Wharton serves on numerous boards, including the Federal Reserve Bank of New York, Ford Motor Company, Time, Inc., Federated Department Stores, and the Aspen Institute. He is a member of the Council on Foreign Relations and the Foreign Policy Association.

From Latin America and the Caribbean

Daniel Oduber (Co-Chairman)

Daniel Oduber was President of Costa Rica from 1974 until 1978. He is currently President of the Governing Board of Costa Rica's National Liberation Party and Vice President of the Socialist International.

Rodrigo Botero (Co-Vice Chairman)

Rodrigo Botero is a private consultant in Bogotá, Colombia. He served as Colombia's Minister of Finance from 1974 to 1976, and was a member of the Brandt Commission on International Development Issues. He is the founder of the Foundation for Higher Education and

Development in Bogotá, and is a member of the boards of the Ford Foundation and the Aspen Institute.

Peggy Antrobus

Peggy Antrobus is Coordinator of the Women and Development Unit at the University of the West Indies in Barbados. She is a founding member of Development Alternatives with Women for a New Era (DAWN), and serves on the boards of the Caribbean Conference of Churches, the International Women's Tribune Center, and other regional and international agencies.

Nicolás Ardito Barletta

Nicolás Ardito Barletta was President of Panama from 1984 to 1985. He was Vice President of the World Bank for Latin America and the Caribbean from 1978 to 1984, and Panama's Minister of Planning and Economic Policy from 1973 to 1978. Dr. Ardito Barletta also served as Director of Economic Affairs at the Organization of American States and President of the Latin American Export Bank.

Guillermo Bueso

Guillermo Bueso, now a private banker, was President of the Central Bank of Honduras. Mr. Bueso has also served as Economic Advisor to the President of Honduras and as Executive Director for Central America at the International Monetary Fund.

Oscar Camilión

Oscar Camilión is serving as a United Nations mediator in Cyprus. He was Argentina's Foreign Minister in 1981 and Ambassador to Brazil from 1976 until 1981. Mr. Camilión has been a professor at the Faculty of Law of the University of Buenos Aires.

Fernando Henrique Cardoso

Fernando Henrique Cardoso is Senator from the State of São Paulo, Brazil. He was the founding President of the Brazilian Center for Analysis and Planning (CEBRAP), and served as President of the International Sociological Association. He is the author of major works on Latin American society and politics.

Roberto Civita

Roberto Civita is President of Editora Abril, Brazil's largest publishing concern. He is Publisher of *Veja*, and a member of the boards of Brazil's Audit Bureau of Circulation, São Paulo's Advertising and Marketing School, and the World Wildlife Fund.

Oliver F. Clarke

Oliver F. Clarke is Chairman of the Board and Managing Director of *The Gleaner*, Jamaica's daily newspaper. He has been Chairman of the Caribbean Publishing and Broadcasting Association, Director of the Private Sector Organization of Jamaica, and Treasurer of the Inter-American Press Association.

José María Dagnino Pastore

José María Dagnino Pastore is Professor of Economics at the Catholic University of Argentina. He has served as Minister of Finance, Minister of Economy and Labor, and Secretary of the National Development Council of Argentina. He has been Vice President of the Foundation for Latin American Economic Research, Ambassador in Europe, and Chairman of the Argentine Investment Bank.

Alejandro Foxley

Alejandro Foxley is President of the Corporation for Latin American Economic Research (CIEPLAN) in Santiago, Chile, and Helen Kellogg Professor of Economics and International Development at the University of Notre Dame. He is the author of many books and articles on economic and political issues.

Carlos Fuentes

Carlos Fuentes is one of Latin America's leading novelists and political commentators. From 1975 to 1977, Mr Fuentes served as Mexico's Ambassador to France. He is currently a professor at Harvard University.

Florángela Gómez Ordoñez

Florángela Gómez Ordoñez is President of the Banco Popular of Colombia. From 1982 to 1984, she served as

Vice Minister of Public Finance and as a member of the President's Council of Economic Advisors.

Xabier Gorostiaga

Xabier Gorostiaga, S.J., is the Director of the Regional Center for Economic and Social Research (CRIES) in Managua, Nicaragua. From 1979 to 1981, he was Director of National Planning for Nicaragua. Father Gorostiaga was the founding Director of the Panamanian Center for Social Studies and Action, and an economic advisor to Panama during the negotiations on the Panama Canal Treaties.

Osvaldo Hurtado Larrea

Osvaldo Hurtado Larrea was President of Ecuador from 1981 to 1984. He is now President of CORDES, the Ecuadoran Corporation for Development Studies. He was founder of the Christian Democratic Party in Ecuador and is currently President of the Christian Democratic Organization of America (ODCA). Dr. Hurtado is a Professor of Political Science at the Catholic University in Quito, and the author of several publications, including *Political Power in Ecuador.*

Elsa Kelly

Elsa Kelly is the Argentine Ambassador to the United Nations Education, Science, and Culture Organization (UNESCO). Dr. Kelly served as Deputy Foreign Minister in Argentina from 1983 to 1985. She was the Alternate Chief of the Argentine delegation to the third United Nations' Law of the Sea Conference. She has been a professor of international law in Argentina.

Pedro-Pablo Kuczynski

Pedro-Pablo Kuczynski is Co-Chairman of First Boston International. He was Peru's Minister of Energy and Mines from 1980 to 1982. From 1976 to 1980, he was President of Halco, a mining corporation. He writes widely on international economic issues, and his most recent book is *Latin American Debt.*

Celso Lafer

Celso Lafer is a member of the board of Metal Leve, S.A., Indústria e Comércio, Brazil and Professor of Public International Law and Jurisprudence at the University of São Paulo.

Augustín F. Legorreta

Augustín F. Legorreta is a Mexican financier and industrialist. He has been Board Chairman and President of Financiera Banamex and the Banco Nacional de México. He has also been President of the Mexican Bankers' Association.

Fernando Léniz

Fernando Léniz is chairman of several major companies in Chile. He is also Professor of Engineering at the University of Chile and President of the Chilean Society of Engineers. From 1973 to 1975, he served as Finance Minister of Chile.

José Francisco Peña Gómez

José Francisco Peña Gómez is the former Mayor of Santo Domingo. He was one of the founders of the Dominican Republic's Dominican Revolutionary Party and served for many years as its Secretary General. From 1978 to 1982, he was Vice President of the Socialist International.

Alberto Quirós C.

Alberto Quirós C. is the President and Editor of *Diario de Caracas*, a leading Venezuelan newspaper. Previously, he was Director of El Nacional. He has been President of Maraven, S.A. and Lagoven, S.A., both operating companies of Petróleos de Venezuela, S.A. He was earlier President of Compañía Shell de Venezuela.

Augusto Ramírez Ocampo

Augusto Ramírez Ocampo is the Regional Director for Latin America and Caribbean of the United Nations Development Programme. He served as Colombia's Foreign Minister from 1984 to 1986, and previously as Mayor of Bogotá.

Jesús Silva Herzog

Jesús Silva Herzog is a professor at the National School of Economics and at the Colegio de México. He served as Mexico's Minister of Finance and Public Credit under two successive presidents, from 1982 to 1986. Previously, Mr. Silva Herzog served as Director General of Credit for the Finance Ministry, as Director General of the National Housing Fund Institute for Wage Earners, and as General Manager of the Banco de México, S.A. He has published several books on economics and finance.

Javier Silva Ruete

Javier Silva Ruete is a Senator and President of the Budget Commission of the Peruvian National Congress. He was Minister of Economy and Finance from 1978 to 1980 and Vice President of the Andean Development Corporation from 1976 to 1978. Previously, he was Manager of Peru's Central Reserve Bank and Minister of Agriculture.

Leopoldo Solís

Leopoldo Solís is Chairman of Mexico's Council of Economic Advisors. He is also a member of El Colegio Nacional and a trustee of the International Food Policy Research Institute in Washington, D.C. He was formerly Under Secretary of Commercial Planning and Deputy Governor of the Central Bank of Mexico. Dr. Solís is the author of numerous books, including *Economic Policy Reform in Mexico*.

Julio Sosa Rodríguez

Julio Sosa Rodríguez is President of the Universidad Metropolitana in Caracas. From 1969 to 1972, he served as Venezuela's Ambassador to the United States. He has served on several economic missions for his government. Dr. Sosa Rodríguez is Chairman of Indústrias VENOCO in Venezuela and President of Banco del Orinoco.

Gabriel Valdés S.

Gabriel Valdés S. completed his term as President of Chile's Christian Democratic Party in 1987. From 1974 to 1981, he was the Director for Latin America and the

Caribbean of the United Nations Development Programme. He served as Chile's Minister of Foreign Relations from 1964 until 1970.

Mario Vargas Llosa

Mario Vargas Llosa is one of Latin America's most widely read novelists. His works have been translated into English and many other languages. In 1983 he headed a national commission to investigate the outbreak of violence in the highlands of Peru. His most recent book is *Who Killed Palomino Molero?*.

Dialogue Staff

Abraham F. Lowenthal (Executive Director)

Abraham F. Lowenthal is professor of international relations at the University of Southern California in Los Angeles. From 1977 to 1983, he was the founding Director of the Latin American Program at the Woodrow Wilson International Center for Scholars. His most recent book is *Partners in Conflict: The United States and Latin America.*

Peter Hakim (Staff Director)

Peter Hakim was Vice President for research and evaluation at the Inter-American Foundation from 1982 to 1984. He was a program officer for the Ford Foundation and served as the Foundation's Assistant Representative for the Southern Cone. He has been a visiting lecturer on nutrition policy at MIT and Columbia University. He is author of numerous articles on U.S.-Latin American relations and recently co-edited *Direct to the Poor: Grassroots Development in Latin America.*